C000263155

Margaret's Baking Journey Around The British Isles

by
Margaret Bacon

Photography: Margaret Bacon
Design: Karen Hibberd and Margaret Bacon
Printing: Barnwell Printers

First published in Great Britain in 2008 by

Margaret and Roger Bacon

Copyright © Margaret Bacon Author 2008
Copright © Photography Margaret Bacon 2008
Publishers Margaret and Roger Bacon

Previous Publications:
Margaret's Recipes From Her Tea Rooms
ISBN: 0-9547914-0-1

All rights reserved

No part of this publication may be reproduced, stored in a
retrieval system, or transmitted, in any form or by any means
without the prior written permission of the publisher, nor be
otherwise circulated in any form of binding or cover other than
that in which it is published and without a similar condition
being imposed on the subsequent purchaser.

ISBN: 978-0-9547914-2-1

Photography: Margaret Bacon

Design: Margaret Bacon and Karen Hibberd

Printed and bound in Great Britain
by Barnwell Printers, Aylsham, Norfolk

INTRODUCTION

Since retiring from her tea-rooms, following on from her success in winning the Top Tea Place of Great Britain Award in 2003 and subsequently publishing her first cookery book 'Margaret's Recipes from Her Tea Rooms', Margaret has not stood still.

She appeared in the very popular TV series on Anglia and Sky Three 'Mrs Beeton's Flying Picnic', presented by Annabel Croft. She has written various articles for magazines over the years and occasionally she can be seen giving a live demonstration. She is still passionate about traditional baking and likes nothing more than to encourage others in the pursuit of maintaining our baking traditions.

Margaret decided to make her latest personal project, researching regional recipes around the British Isles, the subject of her second book. Every recipe in the book has been researched, baked, recorded and photographed by Margaret herself, not to mention the fact that she has tasted them all personally. Sometimes changes have been made in the original recipe, if she felt it was necessary to improve it. Some early recipes, in her opinion, appear a little bland due to the limited ingredients available at the time. Many years of baking experience have given her the confidence to do this.

Margaret and her husband Roger have now moved to their new home, a small brick and flint cottage near the North Norfolk Coast. Their previous property in Baconsthorpe has been sold and has reverted to a private farmhouse.

CONTENTS

REFERENCE RECIPES

QUICK CONVERSION GUIDE
THESE CONVERSIONS ARE APPROXIMATE ONLY

DRY MEASURES

METRIC	IMPERIAL
15 g	½ oz
30 g	1 oz
60 g	2 oz
90 g	3 oz
125 g	4 oz (¼ lb)
155 g	5 oz
185 g	6 oz
220 g	7 oz
250 g	8 oz (½ lb)
280 g	9 oz
315 g	10 oz
345 g	11 oz
375 g	12 oz (¾ lb)
410 g	13 oz
440 g	14 oz
470 g	15 oz
500 g	16 oz (1 lb)
750 g	24 oz (1½ lb)
1 kg	32 oz (2 lb)

LIQUID MEASURES

METRIC	IMPERIAL
30 ml	1 fluid oz
60 ml	2 fluid oz
100 ml	3 fluid oz
125 ml	4 fluid oz
150 ml	5 fluid oz (¼ pint/1 gill)
190 ml	6 fluid oz
250 ml	8 fluid oz
300 ml	10 fluid oz (½ pint)
500 ml	16 fluid oz
600 ml	20 fluid oz (1 pint)
1000 ml (1 litre)	1¾ pints

OVEN TEMPERATURES
THESE TEMPERATURES ARE ONLY A GUIDE

	ºC (CELCSIUS)	ºF (FAHRENHEIT)	GAS MARK
Very Slow	120	250	1
Slow	150	300	2
Moderately Slow	160	325	3
Moderate	180-190	350-375	4
Moderately Hot	200-210	400-425	5
Hot	220-230	450-475	6
Very Hot	240-250	500-525	7

ANGLESEY CAKES

INGREDIENTS

8oz	UNSALTED BUTTER
4oz	CASTER SUGAR
12oz	SELF RAISING FLOUR
½	TEASPOON SALT
6	TABLESPOONS RASPBERRY JAM
1	TABLESPOON ICING SUGAR

METHOD
PRE-HEAT OVEN 180°C/350°F/GAS 4

Mix together the butter and sugar until creamy and smooth.

Gradually work in the flour and salt.

Bring together to form a firm dough and turn on to a lightly floured surface.

Roll out to a thickness of ¼ inch.

Using a 2 inch pastry cutter, cut out 24 rounds re-rolling the dough as necessary.

Cut holes from the middle of 12 rounds using a smaller cutter.

Arrange slightly spaced apart – approximately one inch - on lined baking sheets.

Bake for 10 minutes until risen and golden in colour.

Allow to cool on the baking sheets and then transfer to a cooling rack.

Sandwich the rounds together with jam and dust lightly with icing sugar before serving.

ASHBOURNE GINGERBREAD

In the old days, ginger bread, as it was called since it was served as bread, not cake, was gilded with gold leaf for special occasions. From this custom came the expression 'gilding the gingerbread'.

Ashbourne in Derbyshire has its own gingerbread and the recipe is said to have orginated from French prisoners of war who were kept in the town during the Napoleonic Wars. It is a rich cake, scented with spices and emboldened with delectable black treacle.

GINGERBREAD MEN WERE MADE AND SOLD IN COUNTRY TOWNS AT EASTER FAIRS AND AUTUMN WAKES WEEKS. FASHIONED IN MOULDS THEY WERE DECORATED WITH COLOURED HATS AND SCARLET OR WHITE SUGAR BUTTONS

INGREDIENTS

8oz	SELF-RAISING FLOUR
4oz	SOFT BROWN SUGAR
4oz	BUTTER
1	PINCH SALT
2	TEASPOONS GROUND GINGER
1	TABLESPOON GOLDEN SYRUP
1	TEASPOON MIXED SPICE (optional)

METHOD

PRE-HEAT OVEN 180ºC/350ºF/GAS 4

Sieve the flour, salt and ginger together.

Cream the syrup, butter and sugar in a bowl.

Stir in the dry ingredients.

Knead the mixture on a floured surface to form a smooth dough.

Form into a sausage shape. Press into an oblong and cut into slices.

Place the slices on a lined baking sheet and bake until golden brown.

This will take approximately 30 minutes.

Allow to cool slightly before removing from the tin.

Store in an airtight container

AUDLEY SHORTBREAD

INGREDIENTS

6oz   BUTTER
1½oz ICING SUGAR
8oz   PLAIN FLOUR
1   TABLESPOON
         COCOA POWDER

MAG'S COMMENT:

A GOOD RECIPE FOR
CHILDREN
TO MAKE AND PRESENT
AS A GIFT

METHOD

PRE-HEAT OVEN 160°C/325°F/GAS 3

In a large basin cream together the butter and the icing sugar.

Sift the flour and the cocoa together and gradually add to the butter mixture.

Keep mixing by hand until a soft consistency is reached.

Roll out to approximately ¼ inch and cut into rectangles.

Place on a greased and lined baking tray.

Prick the shortbread with a fork before placing in the oven.

Cook in the oven for approximately 40 minutes.

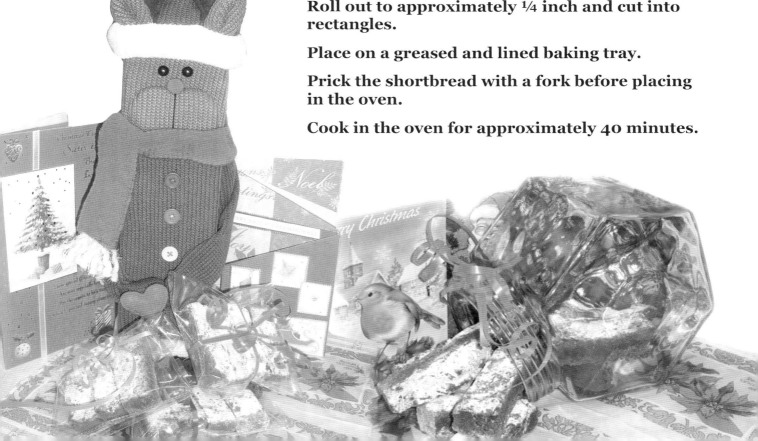

BACONSTHORPE SURPRISE TART

I developed this recipe during the time I ran my tea-rooms in Baconsthorpe.

Not being one to waste food, this tart was the perfect answer when I had surplus cake crumbs.

The 'surprise' comes from the fact that my customers never knew which variety of tart there would be on the menu on any given day.

This recipe shows my 'apricot surprise tart' which was a firm favourite with some of my regular customers. It can be eaten by itself or with cream, custard, or ice cream.

INGREDIENTS

SHORTCRUST PASTRY

12oz **PLAIN FLOUR**
6oz **BUTTER**
COLD WATER TO MIX

FOR THE FILLING

1lb **CAKE CRUMBS**
(for this tart I used crumbs from an apricot and coconut cake)
6 **TABLESPOONS APRICOT JAM**
4oz **PRE-SOAKED DRIED APRICOTS**
1 **TIN CONDENSED MILK (397g)**
10z **DESICCATED COCONUT**
(for sprinkling on top)
2oz **MIXED CHOPPED NUTS (BRAZIL NUTS AND BLANCHED ALMONDS)**
6 **GLACE´ CHERRIES (halved)**

METHOD

PRE-HEAT OVEN 180°C/350°F/GAS 4

TO MAKE THE PASTRY

Sieve the flour into a large bowl and add the butter.

Rub in the butter and mix with cold water to form a stiff paste.

Roll out the pastry and use to line a 10 inch flan dish.

TO MAKE THE FILLING

In a large bowl break the cake into crumbs (I used a food processor).

Add the condensed milk to the crumbs.

Mix thoroughly and put to one side.

Spread the apricot jam in the base of the pastry.

Chop the pre-soaked apricots and sprinkle them on top of the jam.

Cover the jam and the apricots with the cake mixture and press down firmly.

Sprinkle the top with coconut, followed by the chopped nuts.

Decorate the top with the cherries.

Bake in the oven for approximately 1 hour.

Once the tart starts to become golden on top, cover with a piece of greaseproof paper to prevent it from burning.

'SMOKEY' BACON

FOR ADDITIONAL SURPRISE TARTS, SUBSTITUTE THE APRICOT SPONGE CAKE CRUMBS AND APRICOT JAM AS FOLLOWS:

VICTORIA SPONGE CAKE CRUMBS - STRAWBERRY OR RASPBERRY JAM

COFFEE CAKE CRUMBS - MARROW AND GINGER JAM

CHOCOLATE CAKE CRUMBS – LEMON CURD OR STEWED FRUIT

FRUIT CAKE CRUMBS – MINCEMEAT

BAKEWELL PUDDING

Bakewell in Derbyshire is well known for its famous Bakewell Pudding. The recipe is said to have come about by accident because of a misunderstanding between Mrs Graves, Mistress of the White Horse Inn in Bakewell and her cook. A visiting nobleman ordered strawberry tart, but the cook, instead of stirring the egg mixture into the pastry, spread it on top of the jam. Bakewell Puddings are said to be still made today to a secret recipe.

Mag's comment:
I am not sure whether the following recipe is an adaptation of, or the original recipe, but it was given to me many years ago by my mother-in-law (a Derbyshire lady). It is my husband Roger's favourite dessert. He always says it is the 'second' best thing to come out of Derbyshire!!!!!!!!!!! I have made it on numerous occasions and it is always a great success with family and visitors alike.

INGREDIENTS

MAKE THE FLAKY PASTRY RECIPE ON PAGE 151 OR USE ONE PACKET OF FROZEN FLAKY PASTRY

3	TABLESPOONS STRAWBERRY JAM (preferably home-made)
4oz	BUTTER
6oz	CASTER SUGAR
6	EGG YOLKS
3	EGG WHITES
3oz	GROUND ALMONDS
1	TEASPOON ALMOND EXTRACT

LARGE PYREX DISH
10 inches x 1 ½ inches deep

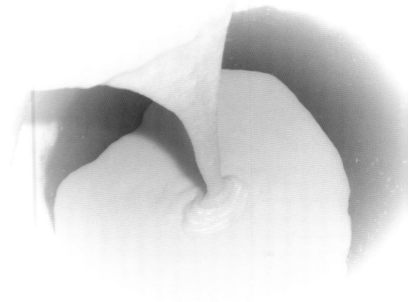

METHOD
PRE-HEAT OVEN 200°C/400°F/GAS 5

Make the flaky pastry and leave in a cool place for one hour before using.

If using frozen pastry, defrost at room temperature.

Roll out the pastry.

Line the dish with the pastry and spread this with the strawberry jam.

In a basin, melt together the butter and sugar.

Mix well.

Carefully blend in the egg yolks and whites and to this add the ground almonds and the almond extract.

Mix thoroughly and pour over the jam into the pastry case.

Bake in a hot oven for approximately 40-50 minutes.

If the top becomes brown before the centre is set, cover the top with a layer of bakewell or greaseproof paper.

This pudding is delicious hot, served straight from the oven.

Serve with fresh pouring cream, or custard.

Mag's tip:

If you prefer to use this recipe with other varieties of jam, raspberry or plum work very well also. I've never tried it with blackcurrant jam, but it's always worth a try.
I love to experiment with different food combinations, otherwise you never know what you might have missed.

BAKEWELL TART

This recipe is a modern version of the 'Bakewell Pudding' which is made with puff pastry and has a custard-like almond filling.

This very popular, tart-like version is simpler to make and is a favourite desert and tea-time treat all over England. I can remember this being served as a school pudding with lots of custard poured over the top.

INGREDIENTS

PASTRY

1lb	PLAIN FLOUR
4oz	MARGARINE OR BUTTER
4oz	WHITE FLORA OR LARD
	COLD WATER TO MIX
	STRAWBERRY JAM
	(approx 2 tablespoons)

SPONGE MIXTURE

6oz	MARGARINE OR BUTTER
6oz	SUGAR (granulated or caster)
6oz	SELF RAISING FLOUR
1	TEASPOON BAKING POWDER
3	LARGE EGGS
1	TEASPOON ALMOND EXTRACT
4oz	FLAKED OR CHOPPED ALMONDS (for decoration – optional)

LARGE PYREX DISH
10 inches diameter x 1 inch deep

METHOD

PRE-HEAT OVEN 180°C/350°F/GAS 4

Combine all the pastry ingredients in the food processor until a soft ball is formed.

Roll out the pastry and line the greased pyrex dish.

Spread the pastry base with the strawberry jam.

Combine all the sponge ingredients in the food processor, knocking down during mixing.

When a soft consistency is reached, pour into the pastry case.

Scatter the almonds on top to decorate.

Bake in the centre of the oven for approximately 1 hour until well cooked.

Cover with greaseproof paper if browning too quickly on top.

DELICIOUS SERVED HOT OR COLD WITH CREAM, ICE CREAM OR CUSTARD

BALMORAL FRUIT CAKE

This recipe was very kindly given to me by a very nice lady, Mrs 'Nan' Graham. I was very fortunate to meet her during a visit to a town called Ecclefechan in Scotland. The purpose of the visit was to find any information I could about the very delicious recipe 'Ecclefechan Butter Tart.' Once ladies start talking about recipes, who knows what information can be hidden away in drawers and cupboards.

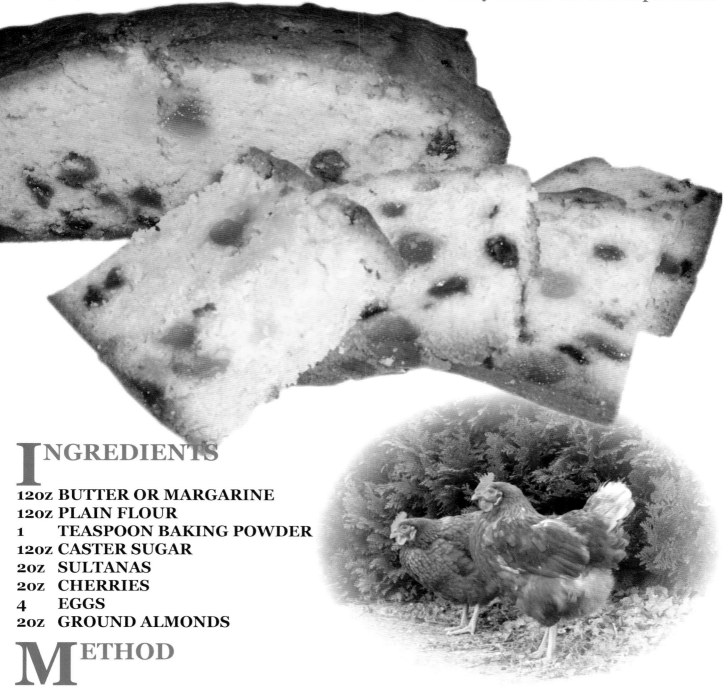

INGREDIENTS

12oz	BUTTER OR MARGARINE
12oz	PLAIN FLOUR
1	TEASPOON BAKING POWDER
12oz	CASTER SUGAR
2oz	SULTANAS
2oz	CHERRIES
4	EGGS
2oz	GROUND ALMONDS

METHOD

PRE-HEAT OVEN 200ºF/400ºC/GAS 5 FOR THE FIRST 30 MINUTES OF COOKING THEN REDUCE THE HEAT TO 375ºF/190ºC/GAS 4 FOR A FURTHER 1 HOUR

Grease and line an 8 inch baking tin.

In a large bowl, cream together the butter and sugar.

Add each egg separately, then add the flour and baking powder.

Add the fruit, chopped cherries and the ground almonds.

Combine all the ingredients well, before putting into the greased and lined baking tin.

BANBURY APPLE PIE

This is a traditional recipe which uses a pie dish with pastry on the top and bottom.

INGREDIENTS

FOR THE PASTRY
12oz	PLAIN FLOUR
5oz	BUTTER
1	TABLESPOON CASTER SUGAR
1	EGG (lightly beaten)

FOR THE FILLING
1½lb	COOKING APPLE (peeled, cored and thinly sliced)
½	LEMON (juice only)
1	ORANGE (zest and juice)
3oz	SOFT LIGHT BROWN SUGAR

PINCH GROUND CINNAMON
PINCH GRATED NUTMEG
MILK TO GLAZE
CASTER SUGAR (for sprinkling)

METHOD

PRE-HEAT OVEN 200ºC/400ºF/GAS 6

TO MAKE THE PASTRY

Put the flour in a bowl and rub in the butter until the mixture resembles fine breadcrumbs.

Stir in the caster sugar, then the egg and enough water to bind the mixture together.

Knead lightly on a lightly floured surface, then roll out two-thirds of the pastry and use to line a shallow 1½ pint pie dish.

Sprinkle the apple slices with lemon juice.

Layer the apples, sultanas, brown sugar, spices and orange zest in the pie dish.

Sprinkle with the orange juice.

Roll out the remaining pastry to form a lid, pressing the edges together.

Scallop the edges, then make a slit in the centre of the pie.

Brush the top with milk to glaze.

BAKE FOR 30 MINUTES UNTIL GOLDEN BROWN

Sprinkle the top with caster sugar and serve hot or cold.

DELICIOUS SERVED WITH THICK CREAM,
POURING CREAM OR ICE CREAM

BANBURY CAKES

INGREDIENTS

1lb 2oz	PUFF PASTRY
2oz	BUTTER
4oz	CURRANTS
1oz	CANDIED PEEL (chopped)
½	TEASPOON GROUND ALLSPICE
½	TEASPOON GRATED NUTMEG
¼	TEASPOON GROUND CINNAMON
2oz	SUGAR (plus a little extra for sprinkling)
1	TABLESPOON RUM
1	EGG WHITE

METHOD

PRE-HEAT OVEN 220°C/425°F/GAS 7

Roll out the pastry thinly and cut into 7 inch circles.

Melt the butter and mix in the remaining ingredients, except the egg white.

Put a spoonful of the mixture in the centre of each circle in a band about 5 inches long.

Bring the pastry round it by pinching the edges over the filling, forming an oval shape.

Cut away any surplus pastry.

Turn them over and press gently to flatten the cakes.

Make three slashes across the top.

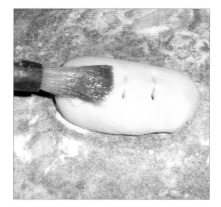

Brush with egg white and sprinkle with sugar.

BAKE FOR 15 MINUTES UNTIL GOLDEN BROWN

These oval cakes, from the Oxfordshire town of Banbury, date back to Tudor times and were originally sold from special lidded baskets and wrapped in white cloths to keep them warm.

Banbury Cakes, are oval cakes of flaky pastry filled with dried currants – so rather similar to an Eccles Cake.

At some point in history the recipe for these cakes changed from its original yeast-risen cake, sounding rather similar to a 'Scottish Black Bun' to the one we know today. They were described as the former in 1615 and as a half-way point in the book 'The Cook's Oracle' by Dr Kitchenen, 1822. He mentions a puff pastry covering, but retains the original yeast dough to hold the fruit in the filling. Lisa Acton's 'Modern Cookery' published in 1845, replaces the yeast centre with a choice of crushed ratafias or macaroons, and suet was added to make a kind of mincemeat.

RIDE A COCK HORSE TO BANBURY CROSS
TO SEE A FINE LADY UPON A WHITE HORSE
WITH RINGS ON HER FINGERS
AND BELLS ON HER TOES
SHE SHALL HAVE MUSIC WHEREVER SHE GOES

BIBURY BLACKBERRY PIE

INGREDIENTS

10oz SHORTCRUST PASTRY
1lb BLACKBERRIES
(rinsed and well drained)
4oz SOFT BROWN SUGAR
½ TEASPOON GROUND
CINNAMON OR NUTMEG
A SMALL PIECE OF BUTTER
(walnut size)
1 TABLESPOON SHERRY

METHOD

PRE-HEAT OVEN 200ºC/400ºF/GAS 6

Roll out the pastry on a lightly floured surface and use half to line a lightly buttered 10 inch pie plate.

Layer the blackberries and the sugar blended with the spice, over the pastry base.

Dot with the butter and then sprinkle on the sherry.

Cover with the remaining pastry, trimming the edges and sealing well.

Decorate with the pastry trimmings.

Brush with a little milk or beaten egg to glaze and cook for about 30-40 minutes or until the pastry is golden.

SERVE HOT WITH CREAM, ICE CREAM OR CUSTARD

English fruit pies are traditionally made either in a pie dish with a deep filling or on a plate with a crust both top and bottom and even sometimes with an extra third pastry layer dividing the fruits inside. A range of fruits can be used such as apples, gooseberries, plums, rhubarb, or as here, blackberries. Pies are always delicious served with custard, whipped cream, pouring cream or ice cream.

BIRSTALL BUNS

INGREDIENTS

1lb	PLAIN FLOUR
2	TEASPOONS SALT
½oz	FRESH YEAST
½	TABLESPOON SUGAR
4floz	MILK AND WATER
2oz	BUTTER
1	EGG (beaten)
3oz	SULTANAS
3oz	CURRANTS
½ oz	CHOPPED CANDIED PEEL

METHOD

Sift together the flour and salt into a large basin.

Cream together the yeast and sugar.

Warm the milk, water and butter together until the butter is melted.

Mix to a smooth dough with the yeast and sugar.

Knead the mixture on a lightly floured board.

Put back into bowl, cover and leave in a warm place to rise.

Knock the dough back when well risen.

Work in the fruits and knead again.

Divide into 12 round buns and leave on a greased or lined baking sheet to prove.

Bake when doubled in size at 220°C/425°F/GAS 7

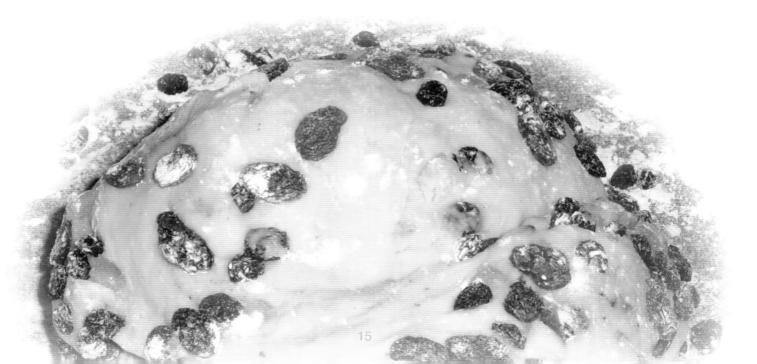

BOLSOVER CAKE

INGREDIENTS

8oz	SELF RAISING FLOUR
½	TEASPOON GROUND NUTMEG
¼	TEASPOON SALT
12oz	BUTTER
7oz	CASTER SUGAR
4	EGGS (beaten)
8oz	RAISINS
8oz	CURRANTS
2oz	MIXED PEEL
2oz	BLANCHED ALMONDS (chopped)
1	TABLESPOON SHERRY

METHOD

Line a 7 inch cake tin with a double thickness of greaseproof paper.

Place thickness of brown paper around the outside of the tin.

PRE-HEAT OVEN 180°C/350°F/GAS 4

Into a bowl sift together the flour, baking powder, nutmeg and salt.

In a mixing bowl cream together the butter and sugar, until light and fluffy.

Gradually beat in the flour mixture and the beaten eggs alternately.

Mix the raisins and currants in a little extra flour.

Add the raisins, currants, peel and chopped almonds, and finally the sherry.

Spoon the mixture into the prepared tin.

Level the surface and make a slight dip in the centre.

Bake in the oven for approximately one hour before reducing the temperature to 160°C/325°F/Gas 3 and continue cooking for a further hour.

ONE RECIPE I CAME ACROSS SUGGESTED
USING A 'SLURP' OF SHERRY!!
I PREFER TO BE A LITTLE MORE PRECISE!!

BORROWDALE TEABREAD

INGREDIENTS

9oz	SELF RAISING FLOUR (wholemeal or white)
9floz	STRONG HOT TEA
½	LEVEL TEASPOON BICARBONATE OF SODA
1	LARGE EGG (beaten)
1lb	MIXED DRIED FRUIT
6oz	SOFT BROWN SUGAR
	GRATED RIND OF 1 ORANGE and 1 LEMON
1oz	MELTED BUTTER
	PINCH OF FRESHLY GROUND NUTMEG

METHOD

Place the fruit in a mixing bowl.

Add the sugar.

Pour on the hot tea.

Stir well, cover and leave overnight.

PRE-HEAT OVEN 160ºC/325ºF/GAS 3

Grease and line a 2lb loaf tin.

To the fruit mixture, add the beaten egg, melted butter, grated rind and the nutmeg.

Mix well.

Sieve the flour and bicarbonate of soda together on to the mixture and fold in until well blended.

Pour into the prepared tin and bake for about 1 hour until firm.

Leave in the tin for 30 minutes before turning out onto a wire rack to finish cooling.

SERVE SLICED, WITH BUTTER

WHEN COLD, KEEP IN A TIN FOR 24 HOURS
TO IMPROVE THE FLAVOUR

BRIGHTON BUTTONS

INGREDIENTS

4oz BUTTER
1oz ICING SUGAR (sieved)
4oz PLAIN FLOUR
FINELY GRATED RIND OF
1 ORANGE
APRICOT JAM

SPRINKLE WITH A
LITTLE ICING SUGAR

METHOD

PRE-HEAT OVEN 180°C/350°F/GAS 4
In a basin cream the butter and icing sugar
together until light and fluffy.

Stir in the flour and beat in the grated orange rind.

Put the mixture into a forcing bag fitted with a
large plain tube.

Pipe small rounds of the mixture on to a greased
and lined baking sheet.

Cook for 15 – 20 minutes.

Remove from the baking tray with a palette knife.

Cool on a wire tray.

When completely cold sandwich the buttons
together with a little of the apricot jam.

BUTTERMERE BISCUITS

As tourism increased in the Lake District, more and more guide books were published. One such book was published by Joseph Palmer in 1792. In the book he described the beauty of the inn keeper's daughter, Mary Robinson, who became known as the Maid of Buttermere.

Visiting the inn became part of the tourists' itinerary. However, she was taken advantage of by a notorious fraudster, who was later hanged for his crimes.

INGREDIENTS

8oz   **PLAIN FLOUR**
4oz   **BUTTER**
3oz   **CASTER SUGAR**
1½ oz **CURRANTS**
GRATED RIND OF ONE LEMON
½   **TEASPOON BAKING POWDER**
1 LARGE EGG (beaten)
PINCH SALT
PINCH OF GROUND CINNAMON

AS AN ALTERNATIVE, REPLACE THE CASTER SUGAR WITH SOFT BROWN SUGAR, OMIT THE LEMON AND CURRANTS, AND ADD 1oz EACH OF CHOCOLATE CHIPS AND HAZELNUTS

METHOD
PRE-HEAT OVEN 180ºC/350ºF/GAS 4

In a large bowl, rub the butter into the flour until it resembles fine breadcrumbs.

Stir in the sugar, currants, lemon rind and baking powder cinnamon and salt.

Mix in the egg, cutting it in with a knife.

When it is evenly mixed, bring it together with your hands.

Extra water should not be needed, but add a little if essential.

Roll out ¼ inch thick and cut out 3 inch circles.

Brush with milk and sprinkle some granulated sugar over the top to finish.

Put the biscuits on a greased and lined baking sheets, and bake for approximately 20 minutes until browned and firm.

CAMBRIDGE BURNT CREAM

Another well known recipe attributed to Cambridge. Cambridge Burnt Cream came to the Trinity College kitchens by way of an enthusiastic nineteenth century academic cook. It is similar to French Creme Brulée.

Frances White, writing in 1932, gives a recipe for tartlets of pastry made with ground almonds filled with cream custard.

Burnt cream, a beautifully rich custard, is served under a layer of caramelised sugar.

INGREDIENTS

1   PINT DOUBLE CREAM
1   TEASPOON VANILLA EXTRACT
4   EGG YOLKS
3   TABLESPOONS SUGAR
    (GRANULATED OR CASTER)

CARE MUST BE TAKEN NOT TO BURN THE CUSTARD

METHOD

Put the cream and vanilla extract in a saucepan and bring to the boil.

Beat the egg yolks in a large mixing bowl with 1 tablespoon of the sugar until they are thick and pale yellow.

Remove the cream from the heat.

Allow to cool slightly, then pour over the egg yolks in a steady stream, whisking constantly.

Transfer the mixture to an ovenproof dish or individual ramekins and bake at 150ºc/300ºf/gas 2 for about 30 minutes, until set.

Leave to cool and refrigerate for about two hours.

Two hours before serving, pre-heat the grill to its highest temperature.

Sprinkle the remaining sugar over the top of the cream, coating the surface evenly and thickly.

Place under the grill as close to the heat as possible and allow the sugar to caramelise to a deep brown.

ALLOW TO COOL AND SERVE CHILLED

CARTMEL CREAM CAKE

INGREDIENTS

6oz   SOFT MARGARINE
6oz   CASTER SUGAR
6oz   SELF-RAISING FLOUR
3   LARGE EGGS (beaten)
PINCH OF SALT

FOR THE SYRUP

3oz   GRANULATED SUGAR
6floz WATER
2   TABLESPOONS RUM
2   TABLESPOONS COFFEE
       ESSENCE

FOR THE DECORATION

½   PINT WHIPPED DOUBLE CREAM
6   GLACE CHERRIES (halved)
HAZELNUTS (chopped)
GRATED CHOCOLATE IN THE CENTRE

METHOD

PRE-HEAT OVEN 180°C/350°F/GAS 4

Grease and line a deep 8 inch round cake tin.

In a large bowl, cream the margarine and sugar well.

Add the beaten eggs and salt.

Sieve in the flour and mix well.

Place the mixture in the tin.

Level the top and bake for about 40 minutes until firm.

Leave in the tin for 15 minutes then turn out on to a large, deep dish.

Meanwhile, heat the sugar and water together in a saucepan
and stir until the sugar has dissolved.

Remove from the heat. Add the rum and coffee essence and stir well.

Prick the top of the cake all over with a skewer and pour the
warm syrup over the warm cake.

Leave the cake for at least 4 hours to absorb the liquid then coat over all
with cream and decorate with cherries, hazelnuts and grated chocolate.

CHELSEA BUNS

Chelsea has been famous for its buns since the eighteenth century. They were originally made in the 'Old Original Bunn House' in Jew's Row. It was the custom in the early days for members of the Royal Family and upper classes to visit the Bunn House in the morning to enjoy coffee and Chelsea Buns. The fame of the buns spread countrywide.

The main characteristics of the Chelsea Bun are the square shape, spiced filling and sweet top.

INGREDIENTS
FOR THE YEAST DOUGH

1oz	FRESH YEAST
2	TEASPOONS CASTER SUGAR
5floz	WATER (1 part boiling to 2 parts cold)
1lb	PLAIN FLOUR
½	TEASPOON SALT
2oz	CASTER SUGAR
4oz	MARGARINE
2	EGGS

METHOD

Cream the yeast and sugar with a little of the warm water.

Mix the flour, salt and sugar in a bowl and rub in the margarine.

Add the yeast liquid and beaten eggs to the flour.

Knead well (either by hand or with a dough hook in a mixer).

Leave to rise in a warm place for 45-60 minutes.

Turn the dough on to a floured surface and knead again lightly.

ADDITIONAL INGREDIENTS

MELTED BUTTER
4oz CASTER SUGAR
8oz CURRANTS OR SULTANAS

Roll the dough into an oblong.

Brush the dough with melted butter.

Sprinkle with the sugar and then the fruit.

Roll the dough up as a swiss roll.

Cut into 1 inch thick slices.

Place the buns in a greased round sandwich tin.

Leave to prove in a warm place for 10-15 miutes.

Bake in a hot oven for 15-20 minutes.

Whilst still warm cover with a warm sugar glaze.

HOW TO MAKE THE SUGAR GLAZE

Place in a saucepan, 4 tablespoons each of milk, water and caster sugar.

Heat gently until the sugar is dissolved, then boil for two minutes.

USE WHILE HOT

CHESHIRE APPLE AMBER

INGREDIENTS

1lb COOKING APPLES
     (Cheshire if available)
4oz CASTER SUGAR
2   LARGE EGGS (separated)
JUICE OF 1 LEMON

METHOD

PRE-HEAT OVEN 180°C/350°F/GAS 4

Peel, core and thinly slice the apples. Add two tablespoons water, and cook, stirring occasionally until they form a puree.

Separate the eggs.

Add 2oz of the sugar, the lemon juice and the egg yolks to the apple, mixing well.

Place in an ovenproof dish and bake for 20 minutes.

Whisk the egg whites until stiff and fold in the remaining sugar.

Pile the meringue evenly on top of the apple mixture.

Return the dish to the oven, and bake for another 10-15 minutes.

DELICIOUS SERVED
HOT OR COLD

CHESTER PUDDING

Chester Pudding is typical of many of the steamed suet puddings found all over the country and is differentiated from the others by its use of blackcurrant jam.

The City of Chester is famous for its half-timbered black and white buildings and Roman city walls. It is also the city of origin for several recipes, including Chester Buns, Chester Cake and Chester Pudding.

INGREDIENTS

4oz SELF RAISING FLOUR
4oz SHREDDED SUET
4oz FRESH WHITE BREADCRUMBS
4oz BLACKCURRANT JAM
1 TEASPOON RUM (optional)
2oz CASTER SUGAR
1 EGG (beaten)
MILK TO MIX

METHOD

Well butter a 2 pint pudding basin.

In a bowl, mix together the flour, suet and breadcrumbs.

Stir together the jam and rum and add to the mixture, combining well.

Stir in the sugar and the beaten egg.

Mix to a soft dough with a little milk, then spoon into the basin.

Cover with greaseproof paper and then kitchen foil, well secured.

Steam for 3 hours, topping up the water as necessary.

Turn out on to a warm dish and serve accompanied by a sauce made of warmed blackcurrant jam, flavoured with a little rum.

CHILTERN HILLS PUDDING

The Chilterns are well known for their villages with attractive brick and flint cottages, clustered around flint churches and nestling in the rolling wooded hills. Some of the villages have historic connections, such as Jordans with its links to the Quaker movement.

INGREDIENTS

2oz   TAPIOCA
¼   PINT MILK
1   TABLESPOON SINGLE CREAM
4oz   SHREDDED SUET
4oz   RAISINS OR SULTANAS
1   TEASPOON BICARBONATE
       OF SODA
       (dissolved with a little milk)
4oz   FRESH WHITE BREADCRUMBS
3oz   SUGAR
A FEW DROPS OF VANILLA ESSENCE

METHOD

TURN OUT ONTO A WARM PLATE
AND SERVE WITH CREAM, CUSTARD,
VANILLA SAUCE OR ICE CREAM

Butter a 2½ pint pudding basin.

In a bowl, soak the tapioca in the milk for 2 hours, then stir in the ceam.

Mix together the suet and the dried fruit.

Stir in the suet mixture, breadcrumbs, sugar and vanilla essence.

Spoon into the basin.

Cover with buttered greaseproof paper.

Seal with kitchen foil.

Steam for 2 ½ to 3 hours, topping up the water as necessary.

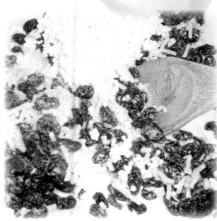

CONNEMARA APPLE TART

In the old days, after the crops had been built into stacks, dried and then brought into the haggard, it was time for the threshing. Entire communities would come together to help each other out and farmer's wives would vie with each other to produce the best feed for the menfolk. Topping off the main course would be apple or rhubarb tart served with big mugs of hot sweet tea.

INGREDIENTS

8oz   SELF RAISING FLOUR
2oz   SUGAR
BRAMLEY OR OTHER GREEN COOKING APPLES
1   EGG (beaten)
2oz   BUTTER
2floz   MILK
PINCH OF SALT
½   TEASPOON GROUND GINGER

TOPPING
¼   TEASPOON CINNAMON
¼   TEASPOON NUTMEG

METHOD

Into a bowl sift the flour, ginger, salt and sugar.

Rub in the fat.

Add milk and eggs to make a soft dough.

Roll out on a floured board.

Cover the base of a greased pie dish with the pastry.

Grate the apples onto the pastry.

Dot with butter.

Sprinkle cinnamon and nutmeg over the top.

Bake in a moderate oven for approximately 30 minutes.

SERVE HOT OR COLD
WITH CUSTARD, CREAM OR ICE CREAM

27

CORNISH FAIRINGS

Traditionally during the week after Christmas, a 'maid-hiring' fair was held in the market town of Launceston, in Cornwall. It was customary to eat or take home ginger flavoured Cornish Fairings.

From late medieval times onwards gingerbreads were made with breadcrumbs and were sold at fairs throughout the country.

Cornish Fairings eventually included ginger biscuits sweetened with honey; coloured with saffron, liquorice, or sandalwood; and decorated with almonds, marzipan, icing or gold leaf.

INGREDIENTS

8oz	PLAIN FLOUR
2	LEVEL TEASPOONS BAKING POWDER
2	LEVEL TEASPOONS BICARBONATE OF SODA
2	LEVEL TEASPOONS GROUND MIXED SPICE
3	LEVEL TEASPOONS GROUND GINGER
1	LEVEL TEASPOON CINNAMON
4oz	BUTTER
4oz	CASTER SUGAR
4	TABLESPOONS GOLDEN SYRUP - gently heated

METHOD

PRE-HEAT OVEN 160°C/325°F/GAS 3

Sieve together the flour, baking powder, bicarbonate of soda, spice, ginger and cinnamon.

Rub in the fat with the fingertips until the mixture resembles breadcrumbs and add the sugar.

Pour in the syrup and mix thoroughly to a fairly stiff paste.

With floured hands, roll the mixture into walnut-sized balls.

Place them on a lined baking sheet, well spaced out to allow room to spread.

Bake in the pre-heated oven for 10-12 minutes, moving the sheet from the top to the bottom of the oven after 5-7 minutes or as soon as the biscuits start to brown.

Leave to cool for a few minutes on the baking sheet before removing to a cooling rack with a spatula, until completely cold.

CORNISH SAFFRON CAKES

Saffron is the dried yellow stigma of the crocus sativum. Over 4,000 flowers are required to produce one ounce of saffron. It is said to be more expensive than gold.

Saffron was introduced to Britain in the 14th century and soon became a popular flavouring.

Crocuses were cultivated in Essex, to meet the demand for saffron. Traditionally they produced a variety of breads, including Essex Huffers.

By the early 15th century the industry in Essex was finished, but saffron continued to arrive from abroad at the cornish ports. Saffron cake, bread and bun recipes remained part of the Cornish tradition, being reserved for special occasions.

(A Cornish saffron-flavoured cake or sweet bread contains currants. It is sometimes made with a yeasted dough, and sometimes risen with eggs and self-raising flour.)

In Britain we tend to use saffron to flavour cakes, rather than adding it to savoury dishes, as is the case in other countries.

INGREDIENTS

¼   **TEASPOON SAFFRON POWDER OR 10-12 SAFFRON STRANDS**
8oz **SELF RAISING FLOUR**
PINCH OF GROUND CINNAMON - (optional)
4oz **BUTTER OR MARGARINE**
4oz **CASTER OR GRANULATED SUGAR**
2oz **CURRANTS**
2oz **SEEDLESS RAISINS**
2oz **CANDIED PEEL – finely chopped**
½   **TEASPOON CARAWAY SEEDS**
1   **EGG**
A LITTLE MILK – to mix

MEASURE THE SAFFRON CAREFULLY, IT IS VERY EXPENSIVE AND THRIFTY CORNISH COOKS WOULD NOT HAVE USED TOO MUCH

METHOD

If using saffron strands, put them into a cup with 1 tablespoon boiling water and leave to stand until the water is cold. (Strain the liquid and use it in place of some of the milk.)

Lightly grease and line 2 baking sheets or trays.

PRE-HEAT OVEN 220°C/425°F/GAS 7

Sift the saffron powder (if used) with the flour, baking powder and cinnamon.

Rub in the butter or margarine.

Add the sugar, dried fruit, candied peel, caraway seeds and the egg.

Mix thoroughly.

Slowly add just enough milk or saffron water to make a sticky consistency.

Put the mixture into 12 small heaps on the sheets or trays, leaving room for the cakes to spread.

Bake for 12-15 minutes or until firm and golden brown on the outside.

CORNISH SWEETHEART TART

INGREDIENTS

6oz SHORTCRUST PASTRY
6oz CASTER SUGAR
6oz BUTTER (melted)
4oz DRIED APRICOTS
     (pre-soaked and chopped)
2oz ROASTED HAZELNUTS
     (chopped)
2   EGGS
2   EGG YOLKS

METHOD

PRE-HEAT OVEN 180°C/350°F/GAS 4

Beat the eggs and yolks with the sugar.

Add the melted butter.

Line a 10 inch baking tin with the pastry.

Scatter the pastry base with chopped apricots and hazelnuts.

Pour in the egg mixture.

Bake for 30-40 minutes, until the crust is rich, golden brown in colour.

SERVE WARM WITH POURING CREAM, CLOTTED CREAM OR ICE CREAM

COVENTRY GODCAKES

During the 16th century it was the custom in Coventry for Godparents to give their Godchildren cakes for good luck at the time of their confirmation. The cakes were usually triangular turnovers whose three points were said to represent the Holy Trinity. The size of the cake denoted the wealth of the giver, and each family tried to outdo the others.

INGREDIENTS

12oz PUFF OR FLAKY PASTRY
8oz MINCEMEAT OR JAM
2   TEASPOONS RUM
     (optional - to mix with the mincemeat)
BEATEN EGG TO SEAL AND GLAZE
GRANULATED SUGAR

SERVE WARM WITH
CREAM, BRANDY BUTTER
OR RUM BUTTER

METHOD

PRE-HEAT OVEN220°C/425°F/GAS 7

Cut the pastry into two equal pieces.

Roll out each piece on a lightly floured board and trim to an oblong about 12 x 8 inches (30 x 20 cm).

Cut each oblong into six 4 inch (10 cm) squares and cut each square diagonally to give two triangles – 24 triangles in all.

Line two baking sheets with greaseproof or bakewell paper and arrange six triangles on each.

Put a teaspoon of mincemeat or jam on the centre of these triangles.

Brush the pastry edges lightly with beaten egg and cover with the remaining triangles.

Press the edges together to seal.

Brush the lids with beaten egg and make three slits in each with a sharp knife.

Dredge each turnover liberally with granulated sugar.

Bake in the centre of the pre-heated oven for 12-15 minutes until golden-brown.

CRANHAM HONEY CAKE

The earliest form of sweetener, honey, has been an important ingredient in cooking throughout history and there have been lots of different recipes baked through the centuries. Its flavour changes in a subtle way according to the type of honey used.

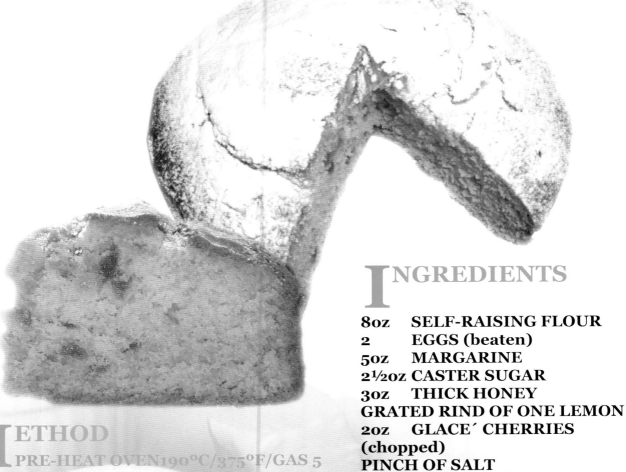

INGREDIENTS

8oz   SELF-RAISING FLOUR
2   EGGS (beaten)
5oz   MARGARINE
2½oz   CASTER SUGAR
3oz   THICK HONEY
GRATED RIND OF ONE LEMON
2oz   GLACE´ CHERRIES (chopped)
PINCH OF SALT
4 TABLESPOONS MILK

METHOD
PRE-HEAT OVEN 190ºC/375ºF/GAS 5

Grease and line a 7 inch round cake tin.

Cream together in a bowl the margarine, sugar and honey.

Beat the eggs and then beat them into the mixture.

Fold in the sieved flour, salt, cherries and lemon rind.

Add the milk and mix well.

Turn into the tin and bake for one hour until golden brown.

ALLOW TO COOL IN THE TIN BEFORE TURNING OUT ON TO A WIRE RACK

CUMBERLAND APPLE PUDDING

INGREDIENTS

1½lb COOKING APPLES
    (peeled, cored and sliced)
SUGAR TO TASTE

8oz   SELF RAISING FLOUR
1   TEASPOON GROUND GINGER
4oz   BUTTER (softened)
4oz   SUGAR

METHOD

PRE-HEAT OVEN 190ºC/375ºF/GAS 5

Butter a large pie dish at least 9½ inches x 7 inches.

Stew the apples with just a very little water and with sufficient sugar to taste.

Put the stewed apples in the pie dish.

Sift the flour, salt and ground ginger into a bowl.

Rub in the butter and stir in the sugar.

Spread the mixture over the apples and bake for about 30 minutes until browned on top.

SERVE HOT WITH
CUSTARD, CREAM OR ICE CREAM

CUMBERLAND CURRANT CAKE

INGREDIENTS

PASTRY

16oz PLAIN FLOUR
5oz BUTTER
5oz LARD
PINCH OF SALT
COLD WATER TO MIX

FILLING

10oz   CURRANTS OR RAISINS
4oz   MIXED PEEL
6oz   COOKING APPLES
5oz   BUTTER
4oz   SOFT DARK BROWN SUGAR
2½floz   RUM
1   TEASPOON ALLSPICE
½   TEASPOON CINNAMON
½   TEASPOON MACE

METHOD

PRE-HEAT OVEN 200ºC/400ºF/GAS 6

Make the pastry in the usual way.

Roll out half and line an oblong tin about 7" x 11" x 1".

Spread the currants or raisins and peel on top.

Peel, core and grate the apples before weighing them, and put them over the currants etc.

Melt the butter, and, off the heat, stir in the remaining ingredients.

Pour over the fruit.

Roll out the remaining pastry and cover the filling.

Brush the pastry over with milk or beaten egg glaze and sprinkle with caster sugar.

EAT HOT AS A PUDDING OR
COLD, CUT INTO
INDIVIDUAL PORTIONS

DELICIOUS SERVED WITH
CREAM, RUM BUTTER
OR CUSTARD

CUMBERLAND PUDDING

INGREDIENTS

3oz SELF RAISING FLOUR
3oz FRESH BREADCRUMBS
3oz SHREDDED SUET
PINCH OF SALT
3oz SOFT BROWN SUGAR
GRATED RIND OF 1 LEMON
1   LARGE COOKING APPLE
1   TABLESPOON
     GOLDEN SYRUP
2   EGGS – beaten

METHOD

Grease a 2 pint pudding basin.

In a large bowl, mix together the flour, breadcrumbs, suet, salt, sugar and lemon rind.

Peel, core and finely chop the apple.

Stir the apple into the flour mixture with the syrup and the eggs.

Mix thoroughly.

Place the mixture in the prepared basin.

Cover with greaseproof paper and foil and steam for 1½ hours.

Carefully turn out of the basin and serve hot.

DELICIOUS SERVED WITH
CUSTARD, CREAM, ICE CREAM OR FOR FOR THAT EXTRA
TREAT LEMON SAUCE

CUMBERLAND RUM BUTTER

Tales of rum smuggling along the Cumberland Coast play a part in the local history of rum butter. One woman, who took a broken cask of the illicit cargo rather than let it be wasted, found that it had dripped into the sugar and butter stored on her larder shelf, and it is said to this, we owe this rich blend of rum and brown sugar with butter and spices.

In Cumberland, rum butter is traditionally served with oatcakes at christening parties. Visitors to see a newborn baby were given rum butter and oatcakes to eat and in return they would leave a silver coin on the day of the christening, when the butter bowl had been emptied, it would be used to hold the coins. A bowl with plenty of buttery coins sticking to it would augur well for the baby's future.

Rum butter is also delicious served with Christmas Pudding, mince pies, and any steamed pudding containing dried fruits.

INGREDIENTS

8oz   SOFT, UNSALTED BUTTER
4oz   SOFT, LIGHT BROWN SUGAR
¼   TEASPOON FRESHLY GRATED NUTMEG
½   TEASPOON LEMON JUICE
3-4   TABLESPOONS RUM

METHOD

Cream the butter until it is fluffy, then beat in the sugar, nutmeg and lemon juice.

Add the rum carefully drop by drop, beating in each drop thoroughly before adding the next so that the butter does not curdle.

CUMBERLAND RUM NICKY

The ports of Whitehaven, Workington and Maryport were at the centre of the UK rum trade, importing rum, molasses and Barbados sugar from the Caribbean in the 18th century.

As a result, spices such as ginger, pepper and nutmeg are now popular ingredients in traditional Cumbrian cooking. Cumberland's flourishing trade with the Far East was sustained from the export of wool for carpet making in exchange for spices.

Historically, 'Nicky' or 'Nickies' seems to have referred to the way they were made - as individual pasties, with a criss-cross cut across the top.

'Nicky' ingredients could vary. It could be made with currants and cinnamon instead of dates and ginger.

Today, Rum Nicky is more often made as a large tart with a pastry lattice top. Whichever way I've made this recipe, it has always been received very favourably by friends and relations.

INGREDIENTS

8oz   DATES
1½oz STEM GINGER (finely chopped)
1oz   DARK SOFT BROWN SUGAR
1½oz BUTTER
2   TABLESPOONS RUM

FOR THE PASTRY
8oz PLAIN FLOUR
4oz BUTTER
 COLD WATER FOR MIXING

METHOD

PRE-HEAT OVEN 190°C/375°F/GAS 5

In a large bowl, rub the butter into the flour.

Add just enough water to made a soft dough.

On a lightly floured surface knead lightly to bring together.

Cover and chill in the fridge whilst preparing the filling.

Chop the dates and stew with 6 tablespoons water in a covered pan.

When soft, mash until smooth.

Add all the other ingredients and mix well.

Roll out two-thirds of the pastry and line a 7 inch flan tin.

Put in the date mixture and spread out evenly.

Roll out the rest of the pastry and cut into thin strips.

Moisten the edge of the pastry in the tin
and arrange the strips in a lattice,
pressing down the ends to keep them in place.

Bake for approximately 25 minutes or until lightly browned.

DEBDEN CHOCOLATE PUDDING

This rich chocolate pudding, invented by a Debden housewife, is said to have taken the area by storm. It creates its own fudge sauce beneath a cake-like top.

INGREDIENTS

4oz	PLAIN FLOUR
2	TEASPOONS BAKING POWDER
¼	TEASPOON SALT
6oz	GRANULATED SUGAR
1oz	PLAIN CHOCOLATE (melted)
2	TABLESPOONS BUTTER (melted)
¼	PINT MILK
2oz	BROWN SUGAR
2oz	CASTER SUGAR
3	TABLESPOONS COCOA
6floz	COLD WATER

METHOD

PRE-HEAT OVEN 170°C/325°F/GAS 3

Sift together the flour, baking powder and salt into a bowl.

Stir in the granulated sugar, melted chocolate and melted butter.

Blend in the milk.

Pour the mixture into a buttered 1½ pint ovenproof dish.

Sprinkle over the top the brown sugar, caster sugar and cocoa in separate layers.

Pour over the cold water.

Bake in the pre-heated oven for one hour.

A layer of chocolate-fudge sauce will form under the sponge topping as the pudding cooks.

Let the pudding cool for an hour before serving.

DELICIOUS SERVED
WITH CREAM OR ICE CREAM

DEPTFORD PUDDING

At one time the northern boundaries of Surrey and Kent were marked by the River Thames, until London extended south of the river. When this recipe was popular, Deptford was a small Surrey village on the Southern bank of the Thames.

INGREDIENTS

6	**SLICES WHITE BREAD** (crusts removed)
2	**EGGS** (separated)
2oz	**SUGAR**
10floz	**MILK**
1	**LEMON** (zest and 2 teaspoons of juice)

METHOD
PRE-HEAT OVEN 180°C/350°F/GAS 4

Make the bread into fine breadcrumbs by grating or using a food processor.

Beat the egg yolks, sugar and milk together in a bowl, then stir in the breadcrumbs, lemon zest and juice.

Whisk the egg whites until they stand up in soft peaks and fold into the mixture, combining thoroughly.

Turn into a buttered 1–1½ pint ovenproof dish and stand the dish in a roasting tin.

Pour in hot water half way up the side of the dish and bake for 30–40 minutes until well risen, set and golden.

SERVE IMMEDIATELY

DERBYSHIRE CHOCOLATE CAKE

The first chocolate arrived in England in the 1500s. The 17th century saw the opening of expensive chocolate houses, which were frequented by the rich and famous. Today chocolate cake is seen on the tea table of every self-respecting household in England.

INGREDIENTS

3oz	COCOA POWDER
4oz	SELF RAISING FLOUR
6oz	MARGARINE OR BUTTER
6oz	CASTER SUGAR
3	EGGS (beaten)
1	TABLESPOON HOT WATER

FOR THE FILLING

2oz	MARGARINE
2oz	COCOA POWDER
4oz	ICING SUGAR

WATER OR MILK TO MIX, IF REQUIRED

FOR THE GLACE´ ICING

6oz	ICING SUGAR
2oz	COCOA POWDER

WATER TO MIX
(approx. 2 tablespoons)

METHOD
PRE-HEAT OVEN 180°C/350°F/GAS 4

Grease and line two 8 inch sandwich tins.

Sieve together the flour and cocoa powder.

Cream the margarine and sugar together in a bowl until light and fluffy.

Beat in the eggs, a little at a time, adding a tablespoon of the flour mixture to prevent curdling.

Fold in the remaining flour and chocolate mixture and stir in the hot water.

Divide the mixture into the tins and smooth the tops.

Bake for 25 minutes until the surface springs back when pressed lightly.

Remove the cakes from the tins and cool on a wire rack.

TO MAKE THE BUTTERCREAM FILLING
Cream the butter.

Sieve the icing sugar and cocoa.

Add to the butter and mix together until smooth and light.

Spread on one of the cakes and sandwich together

TO MAKE THE ICING
Add the water to the sieved icing sugar and cocoa powder to form a thick paste and coat the top of the cake before serving.

43

DERWENTWATER CAKES

The word 'cake' in old recipes would often be referred to items we would call pastries or biscuits today. This recipe is a good example of this, as they can be seen as either a soft biscuit or a firm cake – in any case they are quite delicious.

INGREDIENTS

2	EGGS
4oz	SOFTENED BUTTER
4oz	CASTER SUGAR
8oz	PLAIN FLOUR
4oz	CURRANTS OR CHOCOLATE CHIPS

METHOD

PRE-HEAT OVEN 150ºC/300ºF/GAS 4

Separate the eggs and in a large basin beat the yolks with the butter and sugar.

Add the sifted flour.

When the mixture is crumbly, stir in the currants or chocolate chips.

In a separate bowl, beat the egg whites to a stiff froth and fold in quickly with a metal spoon.

Place dessertspoons of the mixture well apart on greased and lined baking trays, smoothing the tops.

Bake for about 20 minutes until firm to the touch and lightly browned.

DEVON APPLE CAKE

The sweet-acid flavour of this fruity cake is very refreshing.

> COOKING APPLES PRODUCE A VERY MOIST CAKE.
> USE EATING APPLES IF YOU PREFER FOR A SWEETER RESULT

INGREDIENTS

8oz SELF RAISING FLOUR (half white and half wholemeal)
1   TEASPOON GROUND CINNAMON
1   TEASPOON GROUND MIXED SPICE
4oz SOFT BROWN SUGAR
4oz BUTTER
2   LARGE COOKING APPLES (peeled, cored and diced)
2   MEDIUM EGGS
4oz SULTANAS (optional)
A LITTLE MILK (just enough to bind the mixture)

METHOD
PRE-HEAT OVEN 190°C/375°F/GAS 5

Grease and line an 8 inch cake tin.

Mix together all the dry ingredients in a large bowl.

Rub in the butter until the mixture resembles fine breadcrumbs.

Stir in the apples and lastly the egg.

Mix well.

Pour the mixture into the tin.

Bake for 30-40 minutes until risen, firm and golden in colour.

SERVE WARM WITH LOTS OF
CLOTTED CREAM, POURING CREAM OR ICE CREAM

DEVON FLATS

INGREDIENTS

8oz	SELF RAISING FLOUR
4oz	CASTER SUGAR
3½ floz	CLOTTED OR DOUBLE CREAM
1	EGG (beaten)
1	TABLESPOON MILK

METHOD

PRE-HEAT OVEN
220°C/475°F/GAS 7

Mix the flour and sugar together.

Stir in the cream, egg and enough milk to make a stiff dough.
(If the dough feels at all sticky, cover and place in the refrigerator to firm up.)

Roll the dough out on a lightly floured surface until about one-third inch thick, then cut into eight 3 inch rounds using a cutter.

Put onto a greased and lined baking sheet and bake for 8-10 minutes until a light golden brown.

Carefully transfer to a wire rack to cool.

WHEN COLD, STORE IN AN AIRTIGHT CONTAINER

DEVONSHIRE CIDER CAKE

Devon, with its neighbouring county of Somerset, is well known for its cider which gives this cake its distinctive flavour.

INGREDIENTS

4oz	BUTTER
4oz	CASTER SUGAR
2	EGGS
8oz	SELF RAISING FLOUR
1	TEASPOON CINNAMON
½	PINT CIDER

METHOD

PRE-HEAT OVEN 220ºC/475ºF/GAS 7

Grease and line an 8 inch round cake tin.

Cream the sugar and butter together in a bowl until pale in colour.

Stir in the eggs, cinnamon and half of the flour.

Gradually add the cider to this mixture and lastly add the remaining flour and mix thoroughly.

Pour into the tin and bake for approximately 45 minutes until firm to the touch and golden in colour.

DELICIOUS SERVED WITH
CLOTTED CREAM
OR WHIPPED DOUBLE CREAM

DEVONSHIRE SPLITS

The Devonshire Split, that essential item for the perfect cream tea, is a twin to the Cornish Split – it just depends on which side of the Tamar you are.

Traditionally, in the West Country both Devon and Cornish Splits are filled with thick local cream and home-made strawberry jam. Treacle is sometimes used, and then the split is known as a 'thunder and lightening.'

INGREDIENTS

FOR THE FERMENT

1	LARGE EGG (beaten)
7½floz	WARM WATER
10z	FRESH YEAST
4oz	STRONG WHITE FLOUR
½oz	SUGAR

FOR THE DOUGH

14oz	STRONG WHITE FLOUR
¼	TEASPOON SALT
3oz	SUGAR
2oz	BUTTER (soft but not oily)

THE USE OF THE WORD 'SPLIT' TO DESCRIBE A BUN OR ROLL THAT HAS BEEN SPLIT TO RECEIVE JAM, CREAM OR ANOTHER FILLING IS FIRST RECORDED IN 1905 ACCORDING TO THE OXFORD DICTIONARY.

THESE BUNS DID CARRY THE ALTERNATIVE NAME OF 'CHUDLEIGHS' BUT THE REASON FOR THIS IS UNKNOWN. A CATASTROPIC FIRE DID START IN A BAKEHOUSE IN CHUDLEIGH IN 1807 BUT THIS IS SAID TO BE COINCIDENTAL.

METHOD

TO MAKE THE FERMENT

Mix together the beaten egg and enough warm water to give ½ pint of liquid.

Mix the yeast to a smooth paste in 3 tablespoons of the liquid.

Add the rest of the liquid and whisk in the flour and sugar to make a smooth batter.

Cover and put in a warm place to rise for 30 minutes.

TO MAKE THE DOUGH

Sieve the flour and salt on to a working surface or into a large mixing bowl and make a well in the centre.

Put the sugar in the well and pour on the ferment.

Stir to dissolve the sugar, then gradually draw in the flour and mix vigorously to make a soft, sticky dough.

Knead the butter in well until the dough is smooth and silky.

Shape into a ball, put in a warmed and greased bowl, cover with greased polythene and put to rise in a warm place for 45 minutes.

Turn out the risen dough on to a working surface, knock out any bubbles and divide it into 18 equal pieces.

Mould them into balls, cover with a polythene, and leave on the working surface to rest for 5 minutes.

Roll out the balls to make 3 inch discs

Brush any flour off the discs and fold them in half.

Put them on a warmed and greased baking sheet, well spread out.

Cover with greased polythene and put in a warm place to rise for 40 minutes.

PRE-HEAT OVEN 220°C/450°F/GAS 8

Bake for 10 minutes in the pre-heated oven.

When the splits are cool, break them open, fill with jam and cream and dust with icing sugar to serve.

DORNOCH DREAMS

INGREDIENTS

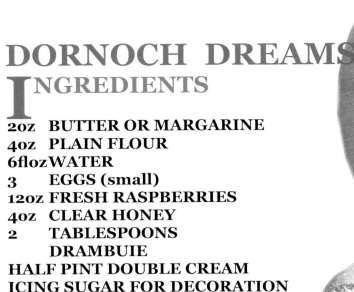

2oz   BUTTER OR MARGARINE
4oz   PLAIN FLOUR
6floz WATER
3   EGGS (small)
12oz FRESH RASPBERRIES
4oz   CLEAR HONEY
2   TABLESPOONS
      DRAMBUIE
HALF PINT DOUBLE CREAM
ICING SUGAR FOR DECORATION

METHOD

PRE-HEAT OVEN 150ºF/300ºC/GAS 2

Place the butter and water in a saucepan and heat until the fat has melted.

Remove from the heat and stir in the flour.

Beat until the mixture forms a ball (and leaves the edges of the pan cleanly).

Beat the eggs and slowly add them, a little at a time, beating well between each addition.

MAG'S TIP:
IF THE MIXTURE APPEARS TOO THIN TO PIPE, ADD A LITTLE EXTRA FLOUR

Spoon the pastry mixture into a large piping bag with a plain nozzle and pipe 12 round cakes onto a lightly greased and lined baking sheet.

Bake in the centre of the oven for 20-30 minutes until golden brown.

Remove from the oven, pierce to allow the steam to escape and then leave to cool.

Mix the raspberries and honey together.

Stir the drambuie into the whipped cream.

Split the buns and fill with the raspberries and cream.

Dust with the icing sugar and serve immediately.

DORSET WIGGS

Traditionally these spiced buns would have been served at breakfast time.

INGREDIENTS

1lb	STRONG WHITE FLOUR
	PINCH OF GROUND CLOVES
	PINCH OF MACE
	PINCH OF NUTMEG
1	TEASPOON CARAWAY SEEDS
2oz	BUTTER
2oz	CASTER SUGAR
½oz	YEAST
½	PINT MILK (warmed)
1	MEDIUM EGG

METHOD

Put the flour, spices and caraway seeds into a large bowl.

Rub in the butter and stir in the sugar.

Mix the yeast to a smooth cream with a little of the warm milk.

Add the yeast mixture, egg and enough of the remaining milk to the dry ingredients to make a soft, elastic dough.

Cover with a clean tea towel and leave to rise in a warm place for approximately 1½ hours until the mixture has doubled in size.

Shape into six large flat buns.

Put on to floured baking trays and leave to rise again for 20 minutes.

PRE-HEAT OVEN 180°C/350°F/GAS 4

Bake for approximately 25 minutes until pale golden in colour.

Transfer to a wire rack to cool.

Serve cold, sliced, with butter.

MAG'S COMMENTS:
AS I DON'T CARE FOR CARAWAY SEEDS, I'D MADE UP MY MIND I
WOULDN'T ENJOY THIS RECIPE - HOW WRONG COULD I BE,
THEY ARE DELICIOUS, SO SOFT

DUFFIELD BATTER PUDDING

INGREDIENTS

4oz FLOUR
1   PINT MILK
1oz MELTED BUTTER
3   EGGS (beaten)
FRESH STEWED FRUIT (as available)

> MAG'S COMMENTS:
> ON THIS OCCASION I USED
> 8OZ COOKING APPLES AND
> 8OZ PLUMS, PLUS ONE
> TABLESPOON DEMARARA SUGAR
> TO SWEETEN THE FRUIT

METHOD

PRE-HEAT OVEN 180ºC/350ºF/GAS 4

Grease an ovenproof dish and spread the drained fruit over the base.

Sieve the flour into a bowl, moisten with a little milk.

Stir in the melted butter and the beaten eggs.

Gradually beat in the remaining milk.

Pour the batter mixture over the fruit and bake for about 50 minutes until set and golden brown.

Serve warm with cream or ice cream.

> MAG'S TIP:
> IF THE PUDDING IS GOLDEN ON THE TOP BUT NOT
> QUITE SET IN THE MIDDLE,
> COVER WITH BAKEWELL PAPER AND CONTINUE TO
> COOK UNTIL SET

DUNDEE CAKE

Dundee Cake is a rich and buttery fruit cake, with a characteristic pattern of blanched almonds on top.

Recipes for this cake go back as far as the 18th century.

Named after the town where it originated, the cake is said to have been a by-product of a marmalade manufacturing plant in Dundee. The availability of orange was incorporated into the cake batter along with sultanas, brown sugar and butter.

INGREDIENTS

6oz	BUTTER
6oz	SOFT BROWN SUGAR
4	EGGS
8oz	PLAIN FLOUR (sifted)
¼	TEASPOON SALT
1oz	GROUND ALMONDS
6oz	SULTANAS
4oz	CURRANTS
2oz	MIXED CHOPPED PEEL
2oz	GLACÉ CHERRIES (rinsed and chopped)
½	LEMON (juice and grated rind)
½	ORANGE (juice and grated rind)
2oz	WHOLE ALMONDS (blanched)

METHOD

PRE-HEAT OVEN 150°F/300°C/GAS 2

Cream the butter and sugar together until light and fluffy.

Beat in the eggs, one at a time.

Fold in the sifted flour, salt and ground almonds and mix well.

Stir in the sultanas, currants, peel, cherries, lemon and orange rind and juice.

Grease a cake tin 7 inches in diameter and line it with a double layer of greaseproof paper.

Spoon the mixture into the tin and smooth the top, hollowing the centre very slightly.

Arrange the blanched almonds on top and bake in the oven for 2 – 2 ½ hours.

Do not open the oven door during the first 30 minutes.

If the cake is browning too quickly towards the end of the cooking time, cover it lightly with a piece of greaseproof paper or foil.

Allow the cake to cool completely before wrapping in foil and storing in an airtight tin, where it could be kept for many weeks – given the chance!

ECCLEFECHAN BUTTER TARTS

Ecclefechan is a small town in Dumfries and Galloway.

This recipe was acquired by the travel writer Bruce Stannard from the Scots Heritage Magazine when he was staying at the Coul House Hotel, as it had so impressed him.

INGREDIENTS

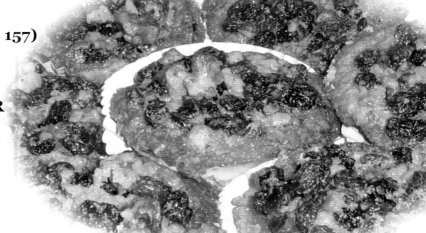

SHORTCRUST PASTRY (see page 157)

2	EGGS (beaten)
4oz	BUTTER (melted)
6oz	SOFT DARK BROWN SUGAR
1	TABLESPOON VINEGAR
8oz	DRIED FRUIT (Mixture of raisins, currants and sultanas)
2oz	CHOPPED WALNUTS

METHOD

PRE-HEAT OVEN 190°C/375°F/GAS 5

Roll out the pastry and line the 12 section patty tins, if making individual tarts or an 7 ½ inch pie dish to make one large tart.

Mix the sugar, butter and beaten eggs together.

Stir in the vinegar.

Add the mixed fruit and the chopped nuts.

Fill the pastry cases with the mixture.

Bake in the oven for approximately 20-30 minutes.

ECCLES CAKES

INGREDIENTS

8oz PUFF OR FLAKY PASTRY
2oz MARGARINE
2oz SUGAR
2oz CURRANTS
2oz SULTANAS
2oz CANDIED PEEL
GRATED RIND AND JUICE OF ONE LEMON
GOOD PINCH MIXED SPICE

METHOD

PRE-HEAT OVEN 220ºC/450ºF/GAS 7

Roll the pastry out until it is about the thickness of a penny.

Cut into large round shapes. (I used a 4 inch plain cutter (not fluted) and this produced very nice sized cakes.)

Cream the margarine and sugar together, then work in all the ingredients.

Put a spoonful of this mixture on one half of the pastry.

Fold over, then press the edges very firmly together.
If necessary brush with a little milk or water to seal them.

Shape with a rolling pin and your fingers until you have round cakes.

Make three splits on the top of each cake.

Brush lightly with milk and caster sugar.

Bake in the centre of a hot oven for about 20 minutes.

If the cakes are becoming too brown reduce the heat or cover with a layer of greaseproof paper.

EGREMONT CAKE

INGREDIENTS

9oz	SELF-RAISING FLOUR
1oz	COCOA POWDER
7oz	CASTER SUGAR
1	LARGE EGG (beaten)
1oz	GOLDEN SYRUP
4oz	MARGARINE OR BUTTER
6floz	TEPID MILK
½	LEVEL TEASPOON

BICARBONATE OF SODA MIXED
WITH 3 floz HOT WATER
PINCH OF SALT
CHOCOLATE BUTTER CREAM (see page 42)

METHOD
PRE-HEAT OVEN 180°C/350°F/GAS 4

Grease and line a 7 inch square deep cake tin.

Into a large bowl, sieve the flour, cocoa and salt.

Add the sugar.

Warm the syrup and margarine/butter until melted.

Add to the flour and mix well.

Add the beaten egg and tepid milk and mix well.

Add the bicarbonate of soda mixture and blend in.

Pour into the prepared tin.

Bake for 30-40 minutes until firm.

Leave in the tin for 15 minutes, then turn out on to a wire rack.

WHEN COLD, CUT ACROSS THE MIDDLE AND
SANDWICH WITH
CHOCOLATE BUTTER CREAM

ENNERDALE CAKE

INGREDIENTS

1	TEASPOON BAKING POWDER
10oz	PLAIN FLOUR
6oz	CASTER SUGAR
6oz	BUTTER
6oz	LARD
1	LARGE EGG (beaten)

PINCH OF SALT
RASPBERRY JAM

METHOD

PRE-HEAT OVEN 180°C/325°F/GAS 3

Grease and line a shallow 7 inch square tin.

Sieve the flour, baking powder and salt into a mixing bowl. Add the sugar.

Cut the butter and lard into small pieces and rub into the flour with the fingertips until it resembles breadcrumbs.

Stir in the beaten egg and knead the mixture until it is well blended.

Roll out half the mixture into a 7 inch square and place in the base of the tin.

Spread with a layer of raspberry jam.

Roll out the remainder of the mixture to a 7 inch square and place on top.

Press the edges with a fork.

Bake for about 50-60 minutes.

Leave in the tin to cool but cut into small squares while still warm.

Sprinkle the top with sieved icing sugar.

ETON MESS

When the annual prize-giving is held at Eton College, one of Britain's most famous public schools, parents and pupils have a picnic on the playing fields. Among the dishes served is this boozy mixture of strawberries, cream and crushed meringue, to which the school has lent its name.

Eton Mess is said to have been served in the 1930's in the school's sock (tuck) shop, and was originally made with either strawberries or banana mixed with ice cream or cream. Meringue was a later addition.

INGREDIENTS

1lb	STRAWBERRIES
12floz	DOUBLE OR WHIPPING CREAM
6	MERINGUES (crushed)
2½floz	KIRSCH
A FEW SPRIGS MINT (optional)	

SERVE IMMEDIATELY

METHOD

Chop and hull the strawberries, reserving a few for decoration.

Place in a bowl and add the kirsch, cover and chill for 2-3 hours.

Whip the cream until it forms soft peaks.

Fold in the strawberries and juices.

Crush the meringue and fold into the mixture.

Spoon into small sundae dishes or wine glasses.

Decorate with the reserved strawberries and a sprig of mint.

EXMOOR FARMER'S CAKE

INGREDIENTS

8oz	CHOPPED DATES
8oz	CASTER SUGAR
3oz	BUTTER
1	TEASPOON BICARBONATE OF SODA
1	EGG (beaten)
1	TEASPOON VANILLA ESSENCE
10oz	PLAIN FLOUR
1	TEASPOON BAKING POWDER
2oz	CHOPPED WALNUTS

FOR THE TOPPING

5	TABLESPOONS LIGHT BROWN SUGAR
2	TABLESPOONS BUTTER
2	TABLESPOONS CREAM

METHOD

PRE-HEAT OVEN 180ºC/350ºF/GAS 4

Pour a breakfast cup of boiling water over the dates and add the bicarbonate of soda.

Stir and allow to cool while mixing the rest of the ingredients.

Combine the two mixtures.

Turn into a greased and lined 10 inch x 10 inch baking tin and cook in a moderate oven for 35 minutes.

Mix together the topping ingredients and boil gently for 3 minutes.

Spread over the cooled cake and sprinkle with walnuts.

FELTON SPICE LOAF

INGREDIENTS

6oz DRIED FRUIT
    (currants, sultanas and raisins)
4oz BUTTER
4oz SOFT LIGHT BROWN SUGAR
4oz SELF RAISING FLOUR
2oz CANDIED PEEL
2oz GROUND ALMONDS
2   EGGS
½   TEASPOON MIXED SPICE
MILK

METHOD

PRE-HEAT OVEN 190ºC/375ºF/GAS 5

In a large bowl, cream the butter, gradually adding the sugar.

Beat until light and fluffy.

Beat the eggs and add a little at a time, whilst continuing to beat.

Fold in the ground almonds.

Gradually fold in the sieved flour and mixed spice to the mixture.

Stir in the finely chopped candied peel and dried fruit.

Add enough milk to produce a soft dropping consistency.

Pour the mixture into a well greased and lined loaf tin.

Smooth the surface.

Bake for 30-40 minutes.

Allow to cool for 5 minutes before removing from the tin.

Turn out on to a wire rack.

GANTON SLAB CAKE

INGREDIENTS

1lb	PLAIN FLOUR
½	TEASPOON SALT
1	LEVEL TABLESPOON BAKING POWDER
1lb	RAISINS
8oz	BUTTER
4oz	GRANULATED SUGAR
1	EGG
TEACUP OF MILK	

METHOD

Grease and line two 1lb loaf tins or a large roasting tin about 10 ins x 7 ins.

Wash the raisins and set to one side.

PRE-HEAT OVEN 160ºC/325ºF/GAS 3

In a large baking bowl, sift the flour with the salt and baking powder.

Rub the butter into the flour and when the mixture resembles fine breadcrumbs, stir in the sugar and raisins.

Beat the egg with the milk and stir them into the dry ingredients with a wooden spoon.

Mix until smooth and then turn the mixture into the prepared tins.

Bake for about 1-1¼ hours if in one tin or ½ - ¾ hour if in two loaf tins.

INGREDIENTS FOR ICING

4oz	ICING SUGAR (sieved)
1	TABLESPOON WARM WATER (flavour to your taste alternately, just use one tablespoon orange juice or lemon juice in place of the water)

METHOD FOR ICING

Place the icing sugar in a basin.

Gradually add the water.

Stir in the flavouring.

The icing should be thick enough to coat the back of a spoon.

Use the icing at once.

THIS IS AN EXTREMELY VERSATILE CAKE. IT IS DELICIOUS HOT STRAIGHT FROM THE OVEN OR COLD FOR PICNICS AND TEA PARTIES. TRY IT BUTTERED, SPRINKLED WITH ICING SUGAR FOR THAT EXTRA SPECIAL TREAT, TRY DECORATING THE CAKE WITH AN ORANGE OR LEMON ICING.

GLOUCESTER PANCAKES

This Cotswold pudding is prepared with a suet dough.
It is the suet that gives them their 'sandy' texture.

INGREDIENTS

6oz FLOUR
PINCH OF SALT
1   LEVEL TEASPOON
        BAKING POWDER
3oz SHREDDED SUET
1   EGG (beaten)
A LITTLE MILK
LARD FOR FRYING

METHOD

Stir together the flour, salt, and baking
powder in a bowl then rub in the suet.

Add the egg and sufficient milk to produce a stiff dough.

Roll out on a lightly floured surface to about ½ inch thick.

Cut into 12 rounds, using a plain, (not fluted) 2 inch cutter.

Put a little lard in a frying pan or griddle and fry the cakes until golden brown on
both sides.

Drain well and serve at once with warmed golden syrup, maple syrup, or a lemon
sauce.

MAG'S COMMENTS:

I DECIDED TODAY TO COOK A FEW
RASPBERRIES WITH THE PANCAKES –
THIS WORKED VERY WELL,
ADDING A LITTLE SHARPNESS TO THE RECIPE.
COULD WORK EQUALLY WELL USING APRICOTS.

GLOUCESTER TARTLETS

INGREDIENTS

6oz   SHORTCRUST PASTRY
2oz   BUTTER (softened)
2oz   SUGAR
A FEW DROPS OF ALMOND EXTRACT
1   EGG (beaten)
2oz   GROUND RICE
RASPBERRY OR APRICOT JAM

METHOD
PRE-HEAT OVEN170ºC/375ºF/GAS 5

Roll out the pastry on a lightly floured surface and use to line about 12 lightly greased and floured patty tins.

In a bowl, cream the butter and sugar together, then stir in the almond extract and the egg.

Fold in the ground rice and combine well.

Place a little jam in each pastry case and top with a good spoonful of the ground rice mixture.

Cook for 15 to 20 minutes or until the filling is golden and springy to the touch.

Cool on a wire rack

Before serving, dust with a little sifted icing sugar.

GOSFORTH GRIDIES

INGREDIENTS

1lb	SELF RAISING FLOUR
1	TEASPOON SALT
8oz	BUTTER
4oz	SUGAR
4oz	CURRANTS
2	EGGS (beaten)
¼	PINT MILK

METHOD

Sift the flour and salt together into a bowl.

Rub in the butter until the mixture resembles fine breadcrumbs.

Stir in the sugar and currants.

Make a well in the centre of the mixture and add the eggs and milk.

Stir the mixture with a round-bladed knife until well combined.

Turn out on to a lightly floured surface and knead lightly.

Roll out to approximately ½ inch thick.

Cut into small rounds and bake on a hot, well-greased griddle or frying pan for 4-5 minutes on each side until golden brown.

> MAG'S TIP:
> FOR THAT ULTIMATE TREAT, SPREAD SOME APRICOT JAM ON TOP

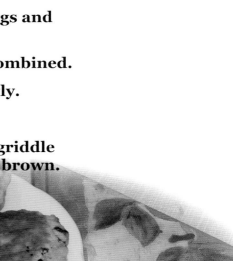

SERVE HOT, WITH BUTTER

GRANTHAM GINGERBREAD

Grantham Gingerbread arose as a result of a 'mistake.' A local baker in the 1740's was making Grantham Whetstones, a flat hard biscuit for travellers. He mistook one ingredient for another and the result became Grantham Gingerbread.

INGREDIENTS

1lb CASTER SUGAR
8oz BUTTER
1   EGG (beaten)
1lb PLAIN FLOUR
½   TEASPOON
BICARBONATE OF SODA
1   TEASPOON BAKING POWDER
½   TEASPOON GROUND GINGER
NUTS & CHERRIES FOR
DECORATION (optional)

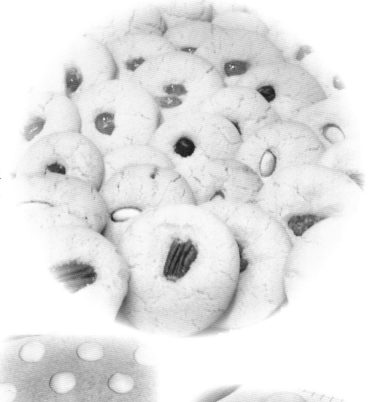

METHOD

PRE-HEAT OVEN 150°C/300°F/GAS 2

Cream the sugar and butter together.

Beat in the egg.

Sift the flour and bicarbonate of soda, baking powder and ground ginger together.

Fold into the creamed mixture.

Make into small balls, or drop teaspoons of the mixture onto a lined baking tray.

Bake for 20-30 minutes or until light brown in colour.

Place on a wire rack to cool.

MAG'S COMMENT:
THESE BISCUITS ARE TRULY DELICIOUS BUT
MAY I SUGGEST TO ANYONE WHO PREFERS A
STRONGER GINGER FLAVOUR, ADD MORE
GROUND GINGER TO THE RECIPE.

GRASMERE CAKE

INGREDIENTS

8oz	PLAIN FLOUR
4oz	BUTTER
4oz	DEMERARA SUGAR
4oz	CURRANTS
2oz	SULTANAS
1	TEASPOON BICARNONATE OF SODA
½	TEASPOON MIXED SPICE
8floz	BUTTERMILK

METHOD

In a large bowl, rub the butter into the flour.

Stir in the remaining dry ingredients, sieving in the mixed spice and bicarbonate of soda.

Pour in the buttermilk and stir with a metal spoon until smooth.

Add more liquid if needed to make a dropping consistency.

Put into a greased and lined 2lb bread tin.

Cover and leave overnight in a cool place.

The next day, bake at 170°c/325°f/gas 3, for one hour, or until cooked through in the centre, and starting to shrink from the sides of the tin.

Cool for a while in the tin before turning out.

THE CAKE MAY BE MADE WITH SOURED MILK INSTEAD OF BUTTERMILK IF THIS IS DIFFICULT TO OBTAIN
TO SOUR THE MILK – STIR A TABLESPOON OF LEMON JUICE INTO FRESH MILK AND LEAVE FOR A FEW MINUTES BEFORE USING

GRASMERE GINGERBREAD

Gingerbread is popular all over the North of England and perhaps the most famous comes from the Lake District village of Grasmere.

The Grasmere Gingerbread Shop still exists and the cake is baked on the premises. The gingerbread has been made to Sarah Nelson's secret recipe since 1854.

The gingerbread was originally made with oatmeal, which was the staple food of Westmorland. Later versions used flour, but it is still more like a shortbread than the traditional cake-type gingerbreads which are better known in the rest of the country.

INGREDIENTS

- 8oz PLAIN FLOUR
- ½ TEASPOON BICARBONATE OF SODA
- ½ TEASPOON CREAM OF TARTAR
- 2 TEASPOONS GROUND GINGER
- 6oz BUTTER (diced)
- 6oz SOFT LIGHT BROWN SUGAR
- 1 LEVEL TABLESPOON GOLDEN SYRUP
- GRANULATED SUGAR (for sprinkling)

METHOD

PRE-HEAT OVEN 170ºC/325ºF/GAS 3

Butter and line an 8 inch sandwich tin.

Place the flour, bicarbonate of soda, cream of tartar and ground ginger in a bowl.

Add the butter and rub in until the mixture resembles find breadcrumbs.

Mix in the brown sugar.

Carefully add the golden syrup and lightly stir into the mixture with a knife.

Spread the mixture in the tin.

Level and bake for 45-50 minutes until golden brown.

Remove from the oven and sprinkle with granulated sugar.

Leave to cool in the tin for 15 minutes.

Cut into twelve wedges and remove from the tin.

Place on a wire rack and leave until cold.

STORE IN AN AIRTIGHT TIN UNTIL REQUIRED

GUILDFORD MANCHETS

The town of Guildford is known for a type of soft, buttery roll called Guildford Manchets. They have been known since the middle ages. Manchet is the medieval term for fine white bread. Traditionally, the rolls are pulled apart when eaten and not cut.

INGREDIENTS

1 lb	STRONG WHITE FLOUR
1	TEASPOON SALT
4oz	BUTTER
3/4oz	FRESH YEAST
1	TEASPOON CASTER SUGAR
5floz	WARM WATER
5floz	WARM MILK
1oz	LARD

GOOD PINCH OF SALT

METHOD

Make the bread dough in the usual way (see page 149) using 1oz of the butter.

After the first rise, knock back and knead until the dough is firm. (This should take about 2 minutes.)

Roll out a rectangle about 6in x 14in.

Cream the remaining butter with the lard.

Add the pinch of salt.

Divide into four pieces.

Place one piece of the creamed butter and lard in the centre of the dough and fold over to enclose the fat.

Seal the edges and roll into a strip.

Repeat this process four times.

Finally, roll out into a rectangle. Cut into 16 pieces and form each into a round. (Mag's comment: Alternatively use a 2 inch cutter.)

Place on greased and lined baking trays. Cover and leave to rise in a warm place for about 20 minutes.

HEAT OVEN 200°C/400°F/GAS 6.

Brush the rolls with milk or beaten egg and bake 30 minutes.

Eat warm with butter.

HAMPSHIRE PICNIC CAKE

INGREDIENTS

4oz	BUTTER
8oz	SOFT BROWN SUGAR
3	EGGS (beaten)
6oz	PLAIN FLOUR or
	PLAIN WHOLEMEAL FLOUR
½	TEASPOON BAKING POWDER
¼	TEASPOON SALT
½	TEASPOON GROUND NUTMEG
¼	TEASPOON GROUND CINNAMON
2	TABLESPOONS MILK
¼	TEASPOON BICARBONATE OF SODA
2	TABLESPOONS CLEAR HONEY
6oz	WALNUT KERNELS –
	6 RESERVED FOR DECORATION -
	THE REST ROUGHLY CHOPPED
6oz	RAISINS OR SULTANAS

METHOD

PRE-HEAT OVEN 170ºC/325ºF/GAS 3

Grease and line a 2lb loaf tin.

Cream the butter and sugar together in a bowl until light and fluffy and beat in a little of the eggs.

Sift the flour, baking powder, salt and spices together, then add alternately to the creamed mixture with the remainder of the eggs.

Warm the milk slightly and stir in the honey, then add the bicarbonate of soda and stir into the mixture.

Add the chopped nuts and dried fruit and combine well together.

Spoon the mixture into the tin and bake for 1½-2 hours, covering the top with bakewell paper if it appears to be browning too quickly.

Place the reserved walnuts on the top of the cake, towards the end of the cooking time.

Cool in the tin for 30 minutes, then turn out on to a wire rack.

HELSTON PUDDING

This fruit pudding originated from Helston and is traditionally served on 'Furry Dance' day in May. The recipe can be used as a light alternative to Christmas Pudding. The Helston Furry Dance is one of the oldest surviving customs in the country. Flora Day is a festival to celebrate the coming of spring and the passing of winter. Its origins are in pagan times. The dances take the form of dignified processions. For the principal dance the gentlemen wear top hats and tails, the ladies in their finest dresses, and the children all in white. This quaint old town is emblazoned with the first greenery of spring, particularly bluebells and hazel.

INGREDIENTS

2oz   SELF RAISING FLOUR
2oz   GROUND RICE
2oz   FRESH BREADCRUMBS
2oz   RAISINS OR SULTANAS
2oz   CURRANTS
2oz   DRIED APRICOTS (chopped)
2oz   SOFT BROWN SUGAR
3oz   SHREDDED SUET
1   TEASPOON GRATED NUTMEG
¼   TEASPOON BICARBONATE OF SODA
MILK (to mix)

METHOD

Sieve the flour.

Mix all the dry ingredients together in a large bowl.

Add milk (enough to form a soft dropping consistency).

Place into a buttered (2 pint) pudding basin.

Cover with greaseproof paper and foil. Tie on tightly.

Place bowl in a large saucepan with boiling water coming half way up the sides of the basin.

Cover the saucepan with a lid.

Steam for 2 hours.

Add more boling water as required.

HEREFORD BRANDY SNAPS

Originally known as 'jumbles' or 'gaufers, meaning wafers, brandy snaps were traditionally sold at fairs. These were a particular feature at the Hereford May Fair.

INGREDIENTS

3oz   BUTTER
4oz   SUGAR
4oz   GOLDEN SYRUP
4oz   FLOUR
½   TEASPOON GROUND GINGER
1   TEASPOON BRANDY
1   TEASPOON LEMON JUICE

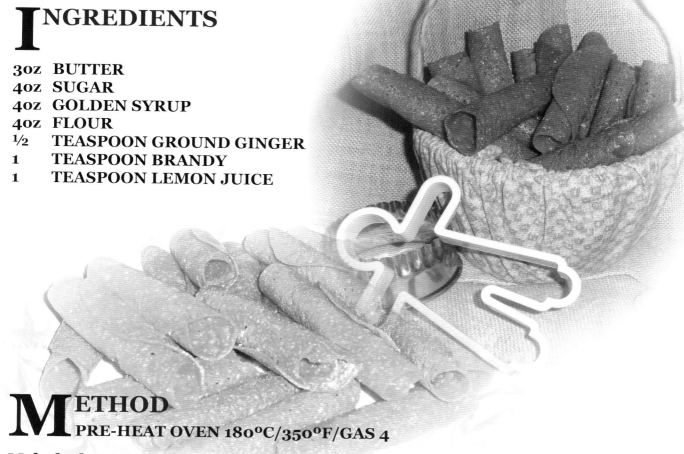

METHOD
PRE-HEAT OVEN 180°C/350°F/GAS 4

Melt the butter, sugar and golden syrup together in a saucepan and leave until cold.

Stir the flour, ginger, brandy and lemon juice into the treacle mixture and combine well.

Drop teaspoons of the mixture on to a well greased and lined baking sheet and bake for 10 minutes until golden in colour.

Allow to cool slightly.

Roll each one round the well-buttered handle of a wooden spoon to form 'rolls' before they set.

The easiest way to do this is to bake the brandy snaps in very small batches.

Allow to cool completely and serve either plain or filled with whipped cream flavoured with brandy.

HEREFORD CIDER CAKE

With the opening of what was to become the world's largest cider-making factory in Hereford in 1887, local cooks began to use the fermented drink in making spicy Cider Cake.

This cake is eaten all the year round as well as at the annual cider festival which takes place in Hereford each June.

INGREDIENTS

6oz	BUTTER OR MARGARINE
6oz	SUGAR
3	EGGS (beaten)
12oz	SELF-RAISING FLOUR (sifted)
1½	TEASPOON BICARBONATE OF SODA
1	LEVEL TEASPOON GRATED

NUTMEG OR POWDERED CINNAMON
10floz CIDER
CASTER SUGAR FOR SPRINKLING

METHOD
PRE-HEAT OVEN 180°C/350°F/GAS 4

Grease and line a rectangular shallow tin 11 inch x 7 ½ inch.

Cream together the butter and sugar until fluffy.

Beat in the eggs.

Fold in half the flour, the bicarbonate of soda and the nutmeg or cinnamon.

Pour the cider into the mixture and mix thoroughly.

Stir in the remaining flour.

Pour the mixture into the prepared tin.

Bake in the pre-heated oven for 35-40 minutes.

Cut into squares when cool and sprinkle with caster sugar.

HIGHLAND CREAMS

INGREDIENTS

8oz   BUTTER OR MARGARINE
3oz   ICING SUGAR
7oz   PLAIN FLOUR
3oz   CORNFLOUR

FOR THE BUTTER CREAM
8oz   BUTTER (softened)
1lb   ICING SUGAR
2   TABLESPOONS HOT WATER
1/2   TEASPOON VANILLA EXTRACT

METHOD
PRE-HEAT OVEN 350ºF/180ºC/GAS 4

Line a baking tray with greaseproof paper.

In a large bowl cream together the butter and icing sugar.

Add the flour and cornflour and mix to a fairly soft consistency.

Push the mixture through a forcing bag and pipe into pyramids or small strips.

Place in the oven and cook for approximately 20 minutes.

When cold, sandwich together with butter cream and dip one end in melted chocolate.

METHOD FOR THE BUTTER CREAM
Cream the butter adding the icing sugar and water gradually.

Add the vanilla essence.

HUNTINGDON PUDDING

INGREDIENTS

6oz   SELF RAISING FLOUR
3oz   SHREDDED SUET
2oz   CASTER SUGAR
5floz MILK
1lb   GREEN GOOSEBERRIES
       (topped and tailed)
2oz   BROWN SUGAR

METHOD

Grease a 2 ½ pint pudding basin.

In a bowl, mix together the flour, suet and caster sugar with sufficient milk to produce a dropping consistency.

Put a layer of pudding mixture in the basin.

Cover with gooseberries and sprinkle with brown sugar.

Repeat and finish with a layer of pudding mixture.

Cover with buttered greaseproof paper.

Finally cover and seal with kitchen foil.

Steam for 2½ - 3 hours, topping up the water as necessary.

Turn the pudding out on to a plate or serve from the basin.

DELICIOUS SERVED WITH
CUSTARD, CREAM OR
ICE CREAM

INVERNESS GINGERNUTS

These biscuits are nice and gingery with extra treacle flavour and crisp texture.

INGREDIENTS

8oz	PLAIN FLOUR
2	TEASPOONS GROUND GINGER
1	TEASPOON GROUND MIXED SPICE
3oz	FINE OATMEAL
3oz	CASTER SUGAR
½	TEASPOON BICARBONATE OF SODA
6oz	TREACLE OR GOLDEN SYRUP
3oz	BUTTER (diced)

METHOD
PRE-HEAT OVEN 325°F/170°C/GAS 3

Put the flour, ginger, spice, oatmeal, sugar and bicarbonate of soda into a bowl and mix together.

Heat the treacle and butter in a small pan until melted.

Pour on to the dry ingredients and mix to make a smooth dough.

Knead well.

Roll the dough out on a lightly floured surface, or if you prefer between two sheets of bakewell or greaseproof paper to approximately ¼ inch thick.

Prick the top with a fork and cut into 2½ inch rounds using a plain cutter.

Put onto a greased and lined baking sheet and bake for 20-25 minutes until firm to the touch.

Transfer to wire racks to cool.

Store in an airtight container.

IPSWICH ALMOND PUDDING

INGREDIENTS

¾	PINT MILK
6oz	GROUND ALMONDS
5floz	DOUBLE CREAM
2oz	FRESH WHITE BREADCRUMBS
2oz	SUGAR
1oz	BUTTER
3	EGGS (beaten)

METHOD

PRE-HEAT OVEN
160°C/300°F/GAS 2

Place the milk and cream in a saucepan, heat but do not allow to boil.

Pour the milk over the breadcrumbs. Stir in the sugar and ground almonds. Allow to soak for 5 minutes.

Add the eggs and mix well.

Pour into a buttered ovenproof dish or individual buttered ramekins.

Dot with knobs of butter.

Place in a bain-marie and bake for 30-40 minutes, or until well set and a golden colour on top.

MAG'S COMMENTS:

THIS IS A VERY LIGHT, DELICATELY FLAVOURED DESSERT. TRY SERVING IT WITH FRUIT OR A DELICATE FRUIT FLAVOURED SAUCE. MY CHOICE WOULD BE APRICOTS.

IPSWICH LEMON PIE

INGREDIENTS

8 oz SHORTCRUST PASTRY
GRATED RIND AND JUICE
OF ONE LEMON
2oz BUTTER
4oz CASTER SUGAR
4   EGGS (beaten)

METHOD

PRE-HEAT OVEN 200°C/400°F/GAS 6

Roll out the pastry on a lightly floured surface and line a greased 7 inch flan dish.

Put the lemon rind and juice, butter and sugar into a saucepan. Heat gently until the sugar has completely dissolved, stirring as little as possible.

Allow the mixture to cool completely. Strain the beaten eggs into it and stir gently until combined.

Pour the mixture into the pastry case and brush the edges of the pie with milk to glaze.

Cook for 10 minutes, then reduce the oven to 180°C/350°F/GAS 4 and cook for a further 15 to 20 minutes, until the filling is set and the pastry is light golden in colour.

SERVE HOT OR COLD WITH CREAM OR ICE CREAM

IRISH APPLE CAKE

INGREDIENTS

3oz BUTTER
3oz CASTER SUGAR
2 EGGS
4oz SELF-RAISING FLOUR
1oz GROUND ALMONDS
½ LEMON (grated rind only)
½ TEASPOON
  VANILLA ESSENCE
2 EATING APPLES

APRICOT GLAZE
2 TABLESPOONS
  APRICOT JAM (sieved)
1 TEASPOON WATER

METHOD

PRE-HEAT OVEN 190ºC/375ºF/GAS 5

Cream the butter and sugar together until light and fluffy.

Add the beaten eggs and sieved flour alternately in two additions, mixing well between each.

Add the ground almonds, lemon rind and vanilla essence.

Pour the mixture into a greased and lined 7½-8 inch tin and flatten out the sponge mixture.

Peel and core the apples, then place wedges of the apples into the sponge mixture.

Bake in the oven for approximately 40-50 minutes.

While still warm and when turned out onto a cooling tray, brush the top with the apricot glaze.

DELICIOUS SERVED WITH A PORTION OF CREAM

IRISH FILLING CAKES

Buttermilk, originally one of the principal ingredients for 'filling cakes' used to be a food for the Irish poor.

In the 18th Century, the Irish satirical writer Jonathan Swift stated that farmers and their families, who paid 'great rents' lived in 'filth and nastiness on buttermilk and potatoes.'

Called 'churn milk,' used with bicarbonate of soda, it helped to lighten the dough. Today, most cooks prefer to make the cakes with ordinary dairy milk, being easier to obtain.

INGREDIENTS FOR THE FILLING

4oz SULTANAS
4oz CURRANTS
2oz SUGAR
½   TEASPOON GRATED NUTMEG OR
     GROUND MIXED SPICE
3   TABLESPOONS WATER

METHOD FOR THE FILLING

Place all the ingredients in a saucepan and bring to the boil.

Simmer for 8-10 minutes stirring occasionally.

Remove the pan from the heat and allow the mixture to cool before being used.

INGREDIENTS

Mag's comments:
I prefer to use the buttermilk

10oz SELF RAISING FLOUR
2oz   SUGAR
½   TEASPOON BICARBONATE OF SODA
½   TEASPOON CREAM OF TARTAR
3oz   BUTTER OR MARGARINE
MILK OR BUTTERMILK FOR MIXING
MILK FOR GLAZING

METHOD
PRE-HEAT OVEN 180ºC/350ºF/GAS 4

To make the cakes, mix the flour and sugar together and add the bicarbonate of soda and cream of tartar, mixing well.

Rub in the margarine with the fingertips until the mixture resembles breadcrumbs.

Gradually mix in just enough milk to make a soft dough.

Roll out into an oblong about 6in wide and about ¼ in thick.

Spread the filling over it to within ¼ in of the edge.

Roll up like a roly-poly, and use a floured knife to cut into ½ in slices.

Place on a greased and lined baking sheet, cut side up and spaced well apart.

Brush over with a little milk and bake in the oven for approximately 20-30 minutes.

IRISH FRAUGHAN SUNDAY CAKE and FRAUGHAN CREAM

In parts of Ireland, the Sunday closest to 1st August is still observed as a Bilberry Feast. Known variously as Fraughan, Garland or Laammas Sunday, it sprang from a Celtic Quarter Day. In some villages, many people still go out for the day.

The Irish favour raw bilberries crushed with sugar and syrup, as an accompaniment for sorbets, ice cream etc.

Bilberries are also known by the names of blaeberries, whimberries, whinberries, whortleberries, fraughans, hurts and hurtleberries in different parts of Great Britain.

INGREDIENTS

8oz	SELF RAISING FLOUR
6oz	GRANULATED OR CASTER SUGAR
6oz	BUTTER
4oz	BILBERRIES (fraughans)
2	EGGS (beaten)
3	TABLESPOONS MILK

FRAUGHAN CREAM

6 floz	WHIPPING CREAM
2oz	BILBERRIES
1	TABLESPOON CASTER OR ICING SUGAR

METHOD

PRE-HEAT OVEN 180°C/350°F/GAS 4

Butter and line a 7 inch round cake tin.

Cream together the butter and sugar until light and fluffy.

Gradually beat in the eggs, adding one tablespoon of flour with the last of the eggs.

Sift the remaining flour and fold in, adding enough milk to produce a stiff mixture.

Gently stir in the bilberries, ensuring they are evenly distributed through the mixture.

Transfer the mixture to the prepared tin.

Bake for one hour.

Remove from the tin onto a rack to cool.

SERVE A SLICE OF CAKE ACCOMPANIED WITH A PORTION OF THE CREAM

FRAUGHAN CREAM

Place the bilberries in a bowl and mash into a juicy pulp.

In a separate bowl whip the cream and caster sugar until stiff.

Fold in the bilberry pulp.

Chill before serving.

IRISH PORTER CAKE

Porter cake is a rich, dark fruit cake which keeps well. The original recipe used porter, a weaker variety of stout, which used to be a very popular working man's pint. It is rarely produced these days, so stout or Guinness make a very good substitute.

INGREDIENTS

8oz SELF RAISING FLOUR
½ TEASPOON BAKING POWDER
4oz BUTTER (softened)
4oz SOFT LIGHT BROWN SUGAR
1 TEASPOON GROUND MIXED SPICE
GRATED ZEST OF ONE LEMON
¼ PINT STOUT OR PORTER
2 EGGS
12oz MIXED DRIED FRUIT

MAG'S COMMENTS:
THE AROMA OF THIS CAKE IS
WONDERFUL BEFORE YOU EVEN
START TO COOK IT

METHOD

PRE-HEAT OVEN
170°C/325°F/GAS 3

Grease and line a deep 7inch cake tin.

Put the flour, baking powder, butter, sugar, spice, lemon rind, stout and eggs in a bowl and beat for 2-3 minutes, until well mixed.

Stir in the dried fruit.

Pour into the prepared tin and bake for approximately 1½ hours or until well risen and firm to the touch.

Leave to cool in the tin.

When the cake is cold, wrap it in greaseproof paper and foil.

Store for one week before eating.

IRISH SODA BREAD

Baking on a griddle or bakestone over the steady glow of a peat fire is said to have given the distinctive flavour to the original irish soda bread. Many homes in Ireland still do some cooking in this way. No yeast is used in this bread. Instead, bicarbonate of soda, cream of tartar and buttermilk give the rise and flavour usually given by yeast.

INGREDIENTS

12oz	WHEATMEAL FLOUR
12oz	PLAIN WHITE FLOUR
1	LEVEL TEASPOON SALT
2oz	LARD
3	LEVEL TEASPOONS BICARBONATE OF SODA
6	LEVEL TEASPOONS CREAM OF TARTAR
2	LEVEL TEASPOONS SUGAR
1	PINT BUTTERMILK

METHOD

PRE-HEAT OVEN 230°C/450°F/GAS 8

Mix together the wheatmeal flour, white flour and salt.

Rub in the lard and then mix in the bicarbonate of soda, Cream of tartar and sugar. Pour in the buttermilk and lightly work up a dough with the hands.

Shape the dough gently into a ball and place it on a lightly greased baking sheet.

Flatten it into a disc about 1 ¼ inch thick.

Cut the disc into quarters and push them apart a little so that there is ¼-½ inch between them.

Dust lightly with wheatmeal flour.

Bake immediately in the pre-heated oven for 30 minutes.

ISLAY LOAF

INGREDIENTS

6oz   RAISINS
6oz   SOFT LIGHT BROWN SUGAR
½   PINT COLD WATER
1   TABLESPOON GOLDEN SYRUP
1oz   BUTTER
10oz SELF RAISING FLOUR (sifted)
2   TEASPOONS BICARBONATE OF SODA
2   TEASPOONS MIXED SPICE
2oz   CHOPPED WALNUTS (optional)

METHOD

In a saucepan, boil together the raisins, sugar, water, golden syrup and butter.

Allow to cool.

PRE-HEAT OVEN 350°F/180°C/GAS 4

When cooled, fold in the flour, bicarbonate of soda, spice and walnuts.

Put into a greased and lined 8 inch cake tin.

Bake for approximately one hour.

DELICIOUS ON ITS OWN OR SPREAD WITH BUTTER

KENT LENT TART

In the days when Lent was strictly observed, many cooks became very ingenious at creating new dishes to break the monotony of their abstenious diet. Sometimes called Kentish Pudding Pie, this recipe is more of a baked cheesecake and was particularly popular in the area around Folkstone.

INGREDIENTS

6oz PLAIN FLOUR
5oz BUTTER
½   PINT MILK
1oz GROUND RICE
2oz SUGAR
2   EGGS
1 LEMON (zest only)
¼   TEASPOON GRATED NUTMEG
1oz CURRANTS

SERVE THE PIE WARM

METHOD
PRE-HEAT OVEN 200°C/400°F/GAS 6

Grease an 8inch fluted flan dish.

Put the flour in a bowl and rub in 3oz of the butter until the mixture resembles fine breadcrumbs.

Stir in 3-4 tablespoons of water to bind the mixture together into a dough.

Roll out the pastry on a floured surface and line the flan dish.

Bake blind for 10-15 minutes.

Reduce the oven temperature to 190°C/375°F/GAS 5.

Put the milk and rice in a pan and bring to the boil, stirring continuously, until the mixture thickens.

Remove the pan from the heat and leave to cool.

When the mixture is cold, cream the remaining butter and sugar together until pale and fluffy.

Beat in the eggs, one at a time, then add the lemon zest, nutmeg and the rice mixture.

Mix thoroughly and pour into the flan case.

Sprinkle the currants on top.

Bake for 40-45 minutes until firm to the touch and golden brown.

KENTISH HUFFKINS

Huffkins are flat, oval loaves, with a deep indentation in the centre of the crust. They have a softer, more open texture than ordinary bread. Eat them sliced at tea time, spread with butter and for that extra treat some delicious home-made jam.

INGREDIENTS

½oz   FRESH YEAST
8floz WARM MILK AND
       WATER MIXED
1lb   PLAIN FLOUR
1   TEASPOON SALT
2   TEASPOONS SUGAR
2oz   BUTTER

METHOD

Blend the yeast with the milk and water.

Leave in a warm place for 15 minutes until frothy.

Put the flour, salt and sugar in a bowl and rub in the butter.

Make a well in the centre, then pour in the yeast liquid.

Beat well together to form a dough that leaves the sides of the bowl clean.

Turn onto a floured surface and knead well for about 10 minutes, until smooth and elastic.

Place in a clean bowl.

Cover with a clean cloth and leave in a warm place for about one hour, until doubled in size.

HEAT OVEN 220°C/425°F/GAS 7

Divide the dough into 12, then roll into oval cakes about ½ inch thick.

Place on 2 greased and lined baking sheets. Cover and leave in a warm place for about 30 minutes, until doubled in size.

Before baking make a deep thumb mark in the centre.

Bake for 15-20 minutes, until golden brown.

Transfer to a wire rack to cool.

To keep the rolls soft wrap them in a tea towel whilst cooling.

LAKELAND FRUIT CAKE

INGREDIENTS

6oz	DESSICATED COCONUT
4oz	CHOPPED DATES
4oz	CHOPPED WALNUTS
4oz	RAISINS
4oz	GLACE` CHERRIES
4oz	MIXED PEEL
2oz	CHOPPED STEM GINGER
4oz	CHOPPED DRIED APRICOTS (pre-soaked)
1	TIN CONDENSED MILK (397g)
1	TEASPOON VANILLA EXTRACT

METHOD
OVEN 150°C/300°F/GAS 2

Grease and line a 7 inch cake tin.

Mix all the ingredients together in a large bowl.

Put the mixture into the cake tin and pack well.

Decorate the top with extra cherries, walnuts and slices of peel.

Bake for 2-2 ½ hours.

Cover the top with a double layer of greaseproof paper if browning too quickly.

WHEN THE CAKE IS COLD, WRAP IN FOIL AND STORE FOR ABOUT 4 WEEKS AS THIS CAKE IMPROVES WITH KEEPING

LAKELAND LEMON CAKE

INGREDIENTS

8oz SELF RAISING FLOUR
6oz BUTTER
6oz CASTER SUGAR
2   LARGE EGGS (beaten)
PINCH OF SALT
PINCH OF GROUND CINNAMON
½   TEASPOON GROUND GINGER
1   LARGE LEMON
      (grated rind and juice)
1   TABLESPOON MILK

MAG'S COMMENTS:
I CHOSE TO FILL MY CAKE WITH HOME-MADE
LEMON CURD. A QUICK AND EFFECTIVE
DECORATION I OFTEN USED IN MY TEA-ROOMS
WAS TO SIMPLY COAT THE TOP OF THE CAKES
WITH EITHER JAM, CURD OR HONEY AND THEN
SPRINKLE THE TOP WITH COCONUT.

METHOD

PRE-HEAT OVEN 170°C/325°F/GAS 3

Grease and line a 7 inch Round cake tin.

In a bowl, cream the butter and sugar until pale and fluffy.

Add the beaten eggs, salt, cinnamon and ginger. Sieve in the flour and mix well.

Add the lemon rind and juice and then add the milk.

Mix well and place in the prepared tin.

Level the top and bake for approximately 1 hour until firm and pale brown.

Leave in the tin for 15 minutes and then transfer to a wire rack.

Keep for 48 hours before cutting.

Serve either plain or cut in half and sandwiched with home-made lemon curd.
If you wish to decorate the top of the cake, simply sprinkle with icing sugar or
place a doily on the top first to create a decorative effect.

LAKELAND SLICE

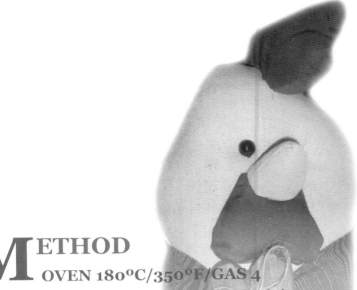

INGREDIENTS

MARZIPAN PASTE

4oz	GROUND ALMONDS
4oz	ICING SUGAR
1	EGG (lightly beaten)

4oz	BUTTER (softened)
4oz	CASTER SUGAR
2	EGGS
8oz	SELF RAISING FLOUR
1	TEASPOON MIXED SPICE
10oz	MIXED VINE FRUIT AND CHERRIES
2½floz	MILK
	FLAKED OR CHOPPED ALMONDS

METHOD

OVEN 180°C/350°F/GAS 4

To make the almond paste sieve the icing sugar into a bowl.

Add the ground almonds and mix with enough egg to make a dough.

Into a large bowl mix together the butter, caster sugar, eggs, flour, spice and fruit.

Add the milk and beat until creamy.

Pour half the mixture into a greased and lined 8 inch/9 inch square tin.

Roll out the almond paste the same size and place on top of the mixture.

Cover the paste with the remaining mix.

Sprinkle the top with chopped almonds and bake for 30-40 minutes or until golden brown and well cooked in the middle.

WHEN COLD,
CUT INTO SLICES

LANCASHIRE FRUIT BRAID

INGREDIENTS

8oz	PUFF PASTRY
8oz	COOKING APPLES
	(peeled, cored and thinly sliced)
10z	CASTER SUGAR
3½oz	LANCASHIRE CHEESE (grated)
3oz	SULTANAS
1	EGG WHITE (beaten) TO GLAZE

BEST SERVED HOT STRAIGHT
FROM THE OVEN FOR THAT
EXTRA TREAT, SERVE
WITH CUMBERLAND BUTTER

METHOD

PRE-HEAT OVEN 220°C/425°F/GAS 7

Roll out the pastry on a lightly floured surface 11 inches square then cut in half on a lined baking sheet.

Lay the apple slices in overlapping rows over the pastry leaving ½ inch border.

Sprinkle over half the sugar, the cheese and sultanas.

Fold the remaining pastry in half and cut slits to within one inch of the edge, half an inch apart. Unfold.

Brush the edges of the pastry with egg white.

Top with remaining pastry and seal the edges.

Bake in the oven for 20 minutes.

Brush with egg white.

Sprinkle with remaining sugar and cook for a further 5-10 minutes.

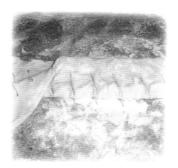

LANCASHIRE HARCAKE

Lancashire Parkin – once known as 'Harcake' or 'Soul Hars cake'. It was originally made to be left for the spirits of the dead returning to their family on All Souls Day. The recipe is now associated with Guy Fawkes Night. Reference is made to this recipe on the 6th November,1800 by Dorothy Wordsworth.

INGREDIENTS

2oz	BUTTER
1lb	FINE OATMEAL
12floz	GOLDEN SYRUP
½oz	GROUND GINGER
1	EGG (beaten)
BROWN ALE	

METHOD

PRE-HEAT OVEN 180ºC/350ºF/GAS 4

Grease and line a deep 10 in x 8 in baking tin.

With fingertips, rub the butter into the oatmeal.

Add the syrup and ginger and combine well.

Add the egg and sufficient ale to make a thick, smooth batter.

Pour the mixture into the prepared tin and cook for 1–1½ hours, until firm and springy to the touch.

If it appears to be browning too quickly, cover the top with foil or greaseproof paper.

Cool in the tin for 5 minutes then turn it out onto a wire rack.

WHEN COMPLETELY COLD, CUT INTO SQUARES AND STORE IN AN AIRTIGHT TIN

LIVERPOOL CHRISTMAS LOAF

This loaf was first baked in the late 1920s as a substitute for Christmas cake as times were very hard for many people. The cake was usually made two weeks before Christmas. After one week, if the finances permitted, ale would be poured over the loaf to improve its texture. Many housewives were too poor to own a cooker and relied upon the local baker to cook their cakes for them, for the cost of a few pence. It was a familiar sight to see poor ladies returning from the bakers with a delicious aroma arising from their newspaper covered cake tins they were carrying.

INGREDIENTS

TWO SMALL LOAVES or ONE LARGE LOAF

FOR THE FERMENT

1	LARGE EGG (beaten)
2 ½floz	WARM MILK
1oz	SUGAR
½ oz	FRESH YEAST

FOR THE DOUGH

4oz	LARD OR COOKING FAT
4oz	SOFT BROWN SUGAR
1	TABLESPOON BLACK TREACLE
1	LARGE EGG (beaten)

FOR THE DOUGH (continued)

8oz	STRONG WHITE FLOUR
1	LEVEL TEASPOON SALT
2	LEVEL TEASPOONS BAKING POWDER
1	LEVEL TEASPOON GRATED NUTMEG
2	LEVEL TEASPOONS GROUND MIXED SPICE
8oz	CURRANTS
4oz	SULTANAS
1oz	MIXED, CHOPPED DRIED PEEL

METHOD

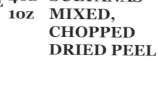

TO PREPARE THE FERMENT

Mix the beaten egg and warm milk together in a large bowl to give ¼ pint of liquid.

Whisk the sugar, yeast and flour into the liquid until thoroughly blended.

Cover with polythene and put to rise in a warm place for 30 minutes.

TO MAKE THE DOUGH

Cream the fat, sugar and treacle together with a wooden spoon in a large mixing bowl until light and fluffy.

Beat the egg into the mixture, then sieve in the flour, salt, baking powder, nutmeg and mixed spice.

Mix together roughly, then pour in the ferment and mix well until the ingredients combine to make a smooth mixture.

Add the currants, sultanas and peel into the mixture until evenly distributed.

Divide the dough in half, and shape each half to fit into a 1lb loaf tin, warmed and well greased.

Cover the tins with greased polythene and put to rise in a warm place for 45 minutes.

HEAT OVEN 400°F/200°C/GAS 6. Bake in the oven for 35-40 minutes.

MAIDSTONE BISCUITS

Scented rose water is an unusual flavouring which was popular with the Tudors.
These biscuits are crunchy and light due to the almond pieces.

INGREDIENTS

4oz BUTTER
4oz CASTER SUGAR
8oz PLAIN FLOUR
2   TEASPOONS ROSE WATER
2oz BLANCHED ALMONDS

METHOD
PRE-HEAT OVEN 180ºC/350ºF/GAS 4

Cream the butter and sugar together, until pale and fluffy.

Fold in the flour, rose water and almonds. Mix together to make a stiff dough.

Place in small heaps on a greased and lined baking sheet.

Bake for 12-15 minutes or until golden brown.

Carefully transfer to wire racks to cool.

MAKES A BAKER'S DOZEN WHEN
COLD, STORE IN AN AIRTIGHT CONTAINER

MALVERN PUDDING

INGREDIENTS

5oz   SELF RAISING FLOUR
5oz   SUGAR
5oz   BUTTER
2oz   CURRANTS
2   SMALL RUSSET APPLES
     (peeled, cored and chopped)
2   EGGS
2-3   TABLESPOONS BRANDY
GRATED RIND OF ONE LEMON

> I was unable to purchase Russet Apples
> so I used Bramley Cooking Apples instead –
> with excellent results

METHOD

Cream the butter and sugar together until soft and light.

Add the beaten eggs.

Fold in the sifted flour and salt.

Gently add the apples, brandy, currants and lemon rind.

Grease a 2 pint pudding basin.

Place a circle of greaseproof paper in the base.

Pour the mixture into the bowl.

Cover the basin with a double layer of greaseproof paper, and a large piece of foil.

Tie tightly with string.

Place the basin in a large saucepan, with water coming half way up the outside of the basin.

Steam the pudding for 1½ - 2 hours, ensuring the water does not evaporate, topping up as needed.

Turn out onto a warmed serving plate and serve hot.

MANCHESTER TART - recipe one

INGREDIENTS

12oz	PUFF PASTRY
4	TABLESPOONS RASPBERRY JAM
4oz	FRESH WHITE BREADCRUMBS
10floz	MILK
1oz	BUTTER (melted)
1oz	CASTER SUGAR
2	EGGS (seperated)
4oz	CASTER SUGAR

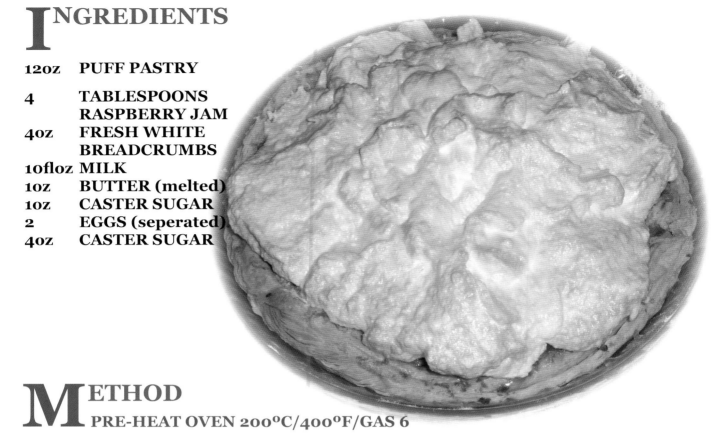

METHOD

PRE-HEAT OVEN 200°C/400°F/GAS 6

Roll out the pastry on a lightly floured surface and use it to line a 10 inch deep flan dish.

Spread the jam over the pastry.

Place the breadcrumbs, butter, 1 oz caster sugar and egg yolks in a large mixing bowl and mix well with a spoon.

Pour the mixture over the jam and bake in the oven for 30 minutes.

Meanwhile, in a clean mixing bowl, whisk the egg whites until stiff, then gradually mix in the ▮▮▮▮ sugar.

Remove the tart from the oven and reduce the temperature to 140°c/275°f/gas 1.

Spread the meringue evenly over the top of the tart.

Return to the oven and cook for a further 30-40 minutes, until the meringue turns a light golden brown.

SERVE HOT, STRAIGHT FROM THE OVEN

MANCHESTER TART - recipe two

This recipe was a very popular school dinner pudding in the 1930s-1970s.

The pudding is still remembered with much affection by past pupils of that time.

I myself remember it very well, although I have to say with some confusion. For some reason, we always referred to it as 'Nottingham Tart!

INGREDIENTS

4oz SHORTCRUST PASTRY

1	PINT MILK
3	TABLESPOONS RASPBERRY JAM
3	TABLESPOONS CUSTARD POWDER
2-3	TABLESPOONS DESICCATED COCONUT
2	TABLESPOONS SUGAR

METHOD
PRE-HEAT OVEN 200°C/400°F/GAS 6

Roll out the pastry and line a baking dish.

Blind bake (prick with a fork and place a piece of greaseproof paper with some baking beans on top of the pastry).

Bake for 15 minutes or until golden brown. Allow to cool.

Spread the jam over the pastry base and sprinkle with some of the coconut.

Heat the milk and whisk into the sugar and custard powder.

Return to the heat and stir gently until the mixture thickens.

Pour gently into the pastry case.

Sprinkle with the remaining coconut to decorate and to prevent a skin forming.

Put back into the oven and leave until the coconut turns golden in colour.

ALLOW TO COOL BEFORE SERVING

MONMOUTH PUDDING

INGREDIENTS

½   PINT MILK
8oz   BREADCRUMBS
4oz   CASTER SUGAR
1oz   SUGAR
1oz   BUTTER (melted)
1   LEMON (grated rind only)
5   TABLESPOONS RASPBERRY
    JAM
2   LARGE EGGS (separated)

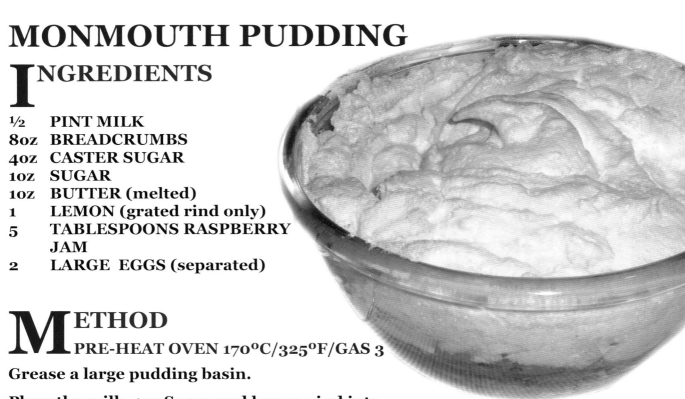

METHOD

PRE-HEAT OVEN 170ºC/325ºF/GAS 3

Grease a large pudding basin.

Place the milk, 1oz Sugar and lemon rind into
a saucepan and bring to the boil.

Pour over the breadcrumbs and allow to stand
for 15 minutes.

Add the melted butter.

SERVE HOT WITH POURING CREAM

Separate the eggs.

Beat the egg yolks into the breadcrumb mixture.

Melt the jam.

Put half the jam into the bottom of the basin.

Pour half the bread mixture over the jam.

Spread the remaining jam over the mixture.

Add the remaining bread mixture.

Bake in the oven for 40-45 minutes.

Whisk the egg whites until they form stiff peaks.

Fold in the caster sugar with a metal spoon.

Spread the meringue over the top of the pudding.

Bake in the oven until the topping is lightly browned.

NEWCASTLE 'SINGING HINNIES'

'Hinny' is a well-known Tyneside corruption of 'honey', and is used as a term of affection.

The ' singing' refers to the contented sound the cake makes as it cooks on a hot griddle or grid-iron.

In the 19th century the cake was a favourite with Geordie children, who ate it at birthday parties. It sometimes had hidden in it pearl buttons, small thimbles and threepenny pieces and these were used to tell the youngsters' fortunes.

A boy who found a button in his piece of cake would be a bachelor for life. A girl who discovered a thimble was destined to be a thrifty housewife. Anyone getting a threepenny piece would be assured that they were going to grow up to be prosperous.

INGREDIENTS

12oz SELF RAISING FLOUR
2oz GROUND RICE
1   TEASPOON SALT
2oz SUGAR
2   TEASPOONS BAKING POWDER
2oz LARD
3oz CURRANTS
¼   PINT CREAM OR HALF CREAM AND HALF MILK

METHOD

Mix together the flour, ground rice, salt, sugar and baking powder.

Rub in the lard with the fingertips until the mixture resembles fine breadcrumbs, then mix in the currants.

Make a well in the centre, pour in the liquid and mix to a soft dough.

Roll out to about ¼ inch thick. Prick all over with a fork and halve or quarter the circle , to make turning over easier.

Bake on a hot greased griddle or greased, heavy- based frying pan for 3-4 minutes on each side until well browned, using a fish slice for turning.

SERVE IT HOT, SPLIT AND BUTTERED

NEWMARKET PUDDING

INGREDIENTS

4	INDIVIDUAL TRIFLE SPONGES
2oz	CUT MIXED PEEL
2oz	SEEDLESS RAISINS
1oz	CURRANTS
7floz	MILK
3	EGGS (beaten)
1	TEASPOON VANILLA ESSENCE
3	TABLESPOONS REDCURRANT JELLY

METHOD

Grease a 5 inch round cake tin or pyrex dish.

Cut the sponges vetically into ½ inch slices.

In a bowl, mix the peel, raisins and currants together.

Put the cake and fruit into the prepared cake tin in alternate layers.

Heat the milk (do not let it boil).

Mix the beaten eggs with the vanilla essence in a bowl and stir in the warm milk.

Pour the custard mixture over the cake and fruit layers.

Leave to stand for one hour.

Half fill a large saucepan with water and bring to the boil.

Cover the top of the cake tin with greased greaseproof paper or foil and tie tightly with string.

Steam the pudding for one hour ensuring the water does not evaporate.

Remove the cooked pudding from the steamer and leave to stand for a few minutes.

Put the redcurrant jelly in a small saucepan and warm through until melted.

Turn the pudding out on to a warmed dish.

Pour the jelly over and serve at once.

NORFOLK APPLE DUMPLINGS

This very substantial dessert is not strictly speaking a 'dumpling' as the apple is encased in shortcrust pastry.

This quintessential British fruit was once thought to have magical powers and, to this day, apples are linked with many English traditions and festivals.

INGREDIENTS

1lb	**SHORTCRUST PASTRY** (see recipe on page 157)
4	**COOKING APPLES** (large and regular in shape)
2	**TABLESPOONS DEMERARA SUGAR**
	SULTANAS (enough to fill the centres of the apples)

METHOD

PRE-HEAT OVEN 200°C/400°F/GAS 5

Peel and core the apples.

Roll out the pastry and divide into four.

Put an apple in the centre of each round of pastry and fill the centre of each apple with sultanas. Sprinkle with the sugar.

Gather the pastry up and seal the apples.

Put the pastry-covered apples onto a greased and lined baking tray.

Decorate the top of the apples with pastry shapes (optional).

Place in the oven and cook until golden.

Reduce the temperature of the oven and continue cooking until the apples are tender.

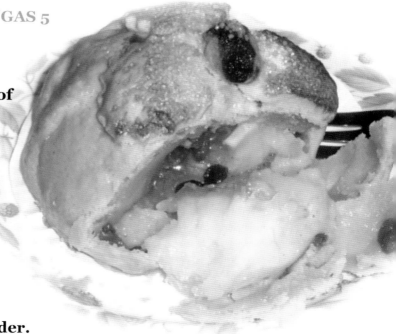

NORFOLK APPLE PIE

INGREDIENTS

12oz	SHORTCRUST PASTRY
2lb	COOKING APPLES
1	DESSERTSPOON LEMON JUICE
1oz	BUTTER
1	TABLESPOON SUGAR
2	TABLESPOONS MARMALADE
20z	CURRANTS OR SULTANAS

BEATEN EGG OR MILK TO GLAZE

METHOD

PRE-HEAT OVEN 200°C/400°F/GAS 6

Roll out the pastry and use half to line a deep 8 inch pie plate.

Peel, core and slice the apples and pour the lemon juice over them.

Melt the butter in a saucepan, add the apples and cook until soft, stirring frequently to prevent them sticking.

Add the sugar, then beat the apples to a pulp.

Place half of the mixture in the pie plate, smooth the marmalade over and sprinkle on the currants or sultanas.

Top with the remaining apple.

Roll out the remaining pastry and use as a lid, sealing the edges well.

Trim and use any left-over pastry to make leaves and shapes to decorate.

Glaze the pie with beaten egg or milk and bake for 15 minutes.

Reduce the oven temperature to 170°C/350°F/GAS 4 for a further 15-20 minutes, or until the pie is golden in colour.

MAG'S TIP:

ORANGE MARMALADE WOULD TRADITIONALLY BE USED IN THIS RECIPE.
I DECIDED TO TRY MY OWN HOME MADE THREE FRUIT (LEMON,ORANGE AND GRAPEFRUIT)
AND THIS WORKED VERY WELL INDEED.
THIS RECIPE WOULD MAKE A WONDERFUL ALTERNATIVE TO MINCE PIES AT CHRISTMAS

NORFOLK FAIR BUTTONS

The button biscuits were traditionally sold at fairs throughout the county.

INGREDIENTS

8oz   FLOUR
4oz   SOFT BROWN SUGAR
1/4oz   GROUND GINGER
PINCH OF BICARBONATE OF SODA
2oz   LARD
4oz   GOLDEN SYRUP

COOL ON A WIRE RACK

METHOD

PRE-HEAT OVEN
180°C/350°F/GAS 4

Mix together the flour, sugar, ginger and bicarbonate of soda and rub in the lard until the mixture resembles fine breadcrumbs.

Add the syrup and mix together thoroughly.

Roll out thinly on a lightly floured surface and cut into 2 inch rounds.

Place on a lined baking sheet and cook for 10-12 minutes.

NORFOLK MILLION PIE

'Million' is the old word for melon, pumpkin or any kind of gourd vegetable. Though this dish is now made with marrow, its original ingredient was pumpkin.

This pie crossed the Atlantic to the New World with the Pilgrim Fathers, who came mostly from East Anglia, and pumpkin pie was served at the Thanksgiving dinner for their first harvest in the New World.

Americans eat the pie at least once a year in honour of their Founding Fathers.

INGREDIENTS

8oz	SHORTCRUST PASTRY
1 lb	PUMPKIN OR VEGETABLE MARROW
	Cut into 1 inch slices (peel, pith and seeds removed)
½	PINT WATER
3oz	APRICOT, PLUM OR GREENGAGE JAM
1	EGG
1½	TABLESPOONS BROWN SUGAR
1	TEASPOON GROUND NUTMEG
2oz	CURRANTS OR RAISINS

SERVE HOT WITH THICK CREAM,
OR COLD ON ITS OWN

METHOD

PRE-HEAT OVEN 200ºC/400ºF/GAS 6

Boil the pumpkin or marrow pieces in the water, stirring occasionally to prevent sticking, until they are soft (about 10 minutes). Drain and cool.

Roll out the pastry and line an 8 inch flan tin or pie plate with it.

Trim the edges of the pastry and keep the trimmings.

Spread the pastry case with a thin layer of jam.

Add the egg, sugar and most of the nutmeg to the cooled pumpkin or marrow and beat together with a fork or in a blender until smooth.

Mix in the dried fruit, then spread the mixture in the pastry case on top of the jam.

Sprinkle with the rest of the nutmeg and lay on a lattice of pastry strips cut from the pastry trimmings.

Bake in the pre-heated oven for 10-15 minutes, then lower the oven temperature to 180ºc/350ºf/gas 4 and cook for a further 15 minutes until the pastry is golden brown.

NORFOLK 'NELSON' SLICES

This recipe is a Norfolk version of bread pudding, named after Admiral Lord Nelson who was a Norfolk man. He was born at Burnham Thorpe, on the north coast, where his father was rector.

INGREDIENTS

1lb	STALE BREAD
3oz	SULTANAS
3oz	RAISINS
4oz	BROWN SUGAR
½	TEASPOON NUTMEG
GRATED RIND OF ½ LEMON	
2	TABLESPOONS ORANGE MARMALADE
3oz	BUTTER (melted)
1	EGG (beaten)
1	TABLESPOON RUM

METHOD

Soak the bread in water for 1 hour.

PRE-HEAT OVEN 200°C/400°F/GAS 6

Squeeze the water out of the bread, then break up any lumps with a fork, until the bread is creamy.

Stir in the dried fruit, then add the rest of the ingredients. Beat well together.

Turn into a buttered and lined, deep pie dish or roasting tin, about 7 - 11 inches, or similar. Bake for 30-40 minutes.

While still hot sprinkle with sugar.

Serve sliced, hot as a pudding, with custard, cream or ice cream.

Can also be served cold as a cake.

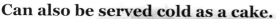

NORFOLK SCONE
INGREDIENTS

1lb	SELF-RAISING FLOUR
2	LEVEL TEASPOONS BAKING POWDER
4oz	BUTTER OR MARGARINE
2oz	GRANULATED OR CASTER SUGAR
2	EGGS (beaten)
¼	PINT MILK

FOR THE FILLING

3oz	SOFT BUTTER
2oz	SOFT BROWN SUGAR
10oz	MIXED FRUIT & PEEL
4	GOOD PINCHES MIXED SPICE

EXTRA MILK AND SUGAR FOR THE TOP

SERVE HOT WITH A GENEROUS PORTION OF THICK CREAM

METHOD
PRE-HEAT OVEN 220°C/450°F/GAS 6

Place all the ingredients except the eggs and milk in a food processor.

Mix for approximately 10 seconds.

Add the eggs and mix for a further 5 seconds.

Next, add the milk gradually until a soft pliable dough is formed.

Turn the mixture onto a floured surface.

Pat down with floured hands.

Divide the scone in two and roll out to approximately ¼ inch thickness.

Place one half on to a large lined baking tray.

Spread with the soft butter. Spread the mixed fruit evenly on top of the butter.

Next sprinkle with the mixed spice.

Finally sprinkle the soft brown sugar.

Roll out the second half of the scone mixture and place on top.

Lighly coat the top with milk and then sprinkle the top with sugar.

Divide the top into portions.

Bake in the oven for 20-25 minutes.

Turn the tray around during cooking.

If the top starts to brown too quickly, cover with a sheet of Bakewell paper.

NORFOLK SHORTCAKES

In country areas it would have been very difficult to satisfy children's appetites for sweet foods as money would have been in short supply. Traditionally, mothers would use bread dough or pastry and wrap it round a little lard from the family pig, with some sugar and dried fruit added before baking. Similarly in the West Country lardy cake and in London the Chelsea Bun were favourites. In Norfolk the pastry version was enjoyed and became a county speciality. Scraps of shortcrust or puff pastry were used after a baking session. The recipe can, of course be prepared with a new dough.

INGREDIENTS

8oz	PLAIN FLOUR
½	TEASPOON BAKING POWDER
PINCH OF SALT	
4oz	LARD
2½floz	WATER
1½oz	GRANULATED SUGAR
1½oz	CURRANTS
CASTER SUGAR FOR SPRINKLING	

METHOD

PRE-HEAT OVEN 200ºC/400ºF/GAS 6

Sieve the flour, baking powder and salt together.

Rub in half the lard until the mixture resembles fine breadcrumbs.

Add the cold water and mix to a dough.

Roll out in a long strip about ½ inch thick.

Divide the lard, sugar and currants into three portions.

Spread one portion of lard on the pastry and sprinkle with one portion of sugar and one portion of currants.

Fold into three layers before giving the pastry a half turn.

Roll out lightly and repeat the process twice more.

Cut into squares and place on a lined baking tray.

Bake in the oven for approximately 15 minutes or until golden brown.

Sprinkle with caster sugar whilst still hot.

Cool and serve freshly baked.

NORFOLK TREACLE TART

This recipe is sometimes called Walpole House Treacle Tart because of its association with the Walpole family of Norfolk.

The name 'treacle tart' can be misleading, since golden syrup, not treacle or molasses is used for the filling. Golden syrup became available only in the late 19th century, making this recipe a relatively recent invention.

This recipe for treacle tart is often known as 'treacle custard' because it does not contain any breadcrumbs like the traditional treacle tart. The filling is rich and creamy and sets into a light lemon-flavoured jelly. It is less sweet and filling than the usual recipe.

INGREDIENTS

8oz	SHORTCRUST PASTRY
7	TABLESPOONS GOLDEN SYRUP
½	LEMON (grated rind and juice)
½oz	BUTTER (melted)
2	TABLESPOONS SINGLE CREAM
2	MEDIUM EGGS (beaten)

METHOD

PRE-HEAT OVEN 180°C/350°F/GAS 4

Grease a 7 inch flan dish and line with the pastry.

Warm the syrup in a saucepan until it 'thins,' then stir in the lemon rind and juice, butter and cream.

Strain the beaten eggs into the mixture and combine gently.

Pour into the pastry case and bake for 35-40 minutes or until the filling is set and lightly golden.

SERVE HOT OR COLD WITH THICK CREAM, CUSTARD OR ICE CREAM

NORFOLK VINEGAR CAKE

INGREDIENTS

8oz	BUTTER	A PERFECT CAKE FOR
1lb	PLAIN FLOUR	A SUMMER PICNIC
8oz	SUGAR	
8oz	RAISINS	
8floz	MILK	
2	TABLESPOONS VINEGAR –	
	WHITE WINE OR CIDER VINEGAR	
1	TEASPOON BICARBONATE OF SODA	

METHOD

Grease and line a 9 inch cake tin.

PRE-HEAT OVEN 180ºC/350ºF/GAS 4

Rub the butter into the flour to give a crumble-like consistency.

Mix in the sugar and the fruit.

Put the milk into a large jug or bowl and add the vinegar.

Add the bicarbonate of soda into the milk and vinegar.

It is wise to hold it over the mixing bowl while doing this in case it froths and spills over.

Stir the liquid into the cake mixture.

Beat well and put into the lined baking tin.

NORTHAMPTONSHIRE SEED CAKE

Traditionally served at sheep shearing time.
A plain cake flavoured with nutmeg and caraway seeds.

INGREDIENTS

8oz	BUTTER
8oz	CASTER SUGAR
4	EGGS
8oz	SELF RAISING FLOUR
½	TEASPOON BAKING POWDER
1	TEASPOON GROUND NUTMEG
1oz	CARAWAY SEEDS

METHOD

PRE-HEAT OVEN 180ºC/350ºF/GAS 4

Grease and line an 8 inch round cake tin.

Cream the butter and sugar together in a bowl until light and fluffy.

Place the eggs in a bowl set over a saucepan of hot water and whisk until fluffy, then whisk into the butter mixture.

Sift the flour and baking powder together and fold into the mixture, together with the nutmeg.

Add the caraway seeds and combine well.

Turn into the prepared tin and smooth over the top.

Bake for 1½ - 2 hours, covering the top with a piece of kitchen foil if it appears to be browning too quickly.

Cool in the tin for 5 minutes before turning on to a wire rack.

NORTHUMBERLAND THRESHING DAY BARLEY BREAD

This is a scone-like bread which was traditionally baked, on a griddle when the harvest was being threshed.

INGREDIENTS

1 lb	BARLEY FLOUR
4oz	PLAIN FLOUR or PLAIN WHOLEMEAL FLOUR
1	TEASPOON SALT
1	TEASPOON BICARBONATE OF SODA
2	TEASPOONS CREAM OF TARTAR
1	PINT BUTTERMILK OR MILK
1	BEATEN EGG

MAG' COMMENTS:
I CAN'T THINK OF ANYTHING MORE INVITING THAN THE SIGHT OF A COTTAGE LOAF ON A TABLE SET FOR TEA.

METHOD

PRE-HEAT OVEN 220°C/450°F/GAS 6

In a large bowl, mix together the flours, salt, bicarbonate of soda and cream of tartar.

Stir in the buttermilk or milk to form a firm dough.

Turn out on to a lightly floured surface and form into a round scone shape.

Brush with the beaten egg and place on a lightly greased and lined baking sheet.

Bake for 30 minutes or until golden.

Serve with butter – delicious with fish, cheese, cold meats or just plain bread and jam – home-made, of course!

NOTTINGHAM PUDDING

The Bramley cooking apple originates from Southwell, Nottinghamshire. The original tree is still flourishing in a garden in the Minster town

INGREDIENTS

6	BRAMLEY APPLES (even size)
3oz	BUTTER
3oz	CASTER SUGAR
	PINCH OF NUTMEG
	PINCH OF CINNAMON
4oz	PLAIN FLOUR
3	EGGS
	WATER
	SALT
	MILK

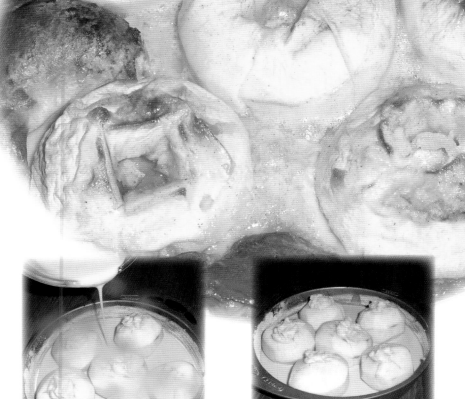

METHOD

PRE-HEAT OVEN 200°C/400°F/GAS 6

Peel and core the apples.

Place in a well-buttered oven-proof dish.

Cream the butter and sugar.

Add the nutmeg and cinnamon.

Fill the centre of each apple with the mixture.

Blend the flour with a little cold water and add the well-beaten eggs to it with a pinch of salt and sufficient milk to make a thick creamy batter.

Pour over the apples and bake at for approximately 50 minutes.

Best eaten hot, straight from the oven.

OXFORD PUDDINGS

I received a letter from Mr J Bootman enclosing some fascinating recipes. In the letter he said "I enclose a few recipes from a pocket book of my great grandmother when she was a cook or housekeeper in Norfolk. They date from 1858 – 1864 and are copied as written, so you may have trouble with some of them, but I am sure you will cope."

Well here goes, I will type them as written and attempt to put them into today's terms.

" Take a quarter of a pound of grated biscuit, the same quantity of currants the same of suet finely chopped, a spoonful of sugar and a little nutmeg, mix them together, take the yolks of three eggs and make up the puddings into balls. Fry them a light colour in fresh butter and serve with white wine sauce."

INGREDIENTS

IN TODAY'S TERMS

4oz BISCUIT CRUMBS
     (I used Digestive biscuits)
4oz CURRANTS
4oz SUET (finely chopped)
1   DESSERTSPOON OF SOFT
     BROWN SUGAR
½   TEASPOON OF NUTMEG
3   LARGE EGG YOLKS
BUTTER FOR FRYING

METHOD

Put the biscuit crumbs, currants, suet, sugar and nutmeg into a large basin and mix well.

Beat the egg yolks and add to the mixture.

Mix well together. I found it easier to use my hands to combine the mixture.

Divide the mixture into balls.

Heat the butter gently in a frying pan.

Add the balls and fry gently until a light golden colour.

PRESTON GINGERBREAD

Preston Gingerbread is much drier and crunchier than the soft gingerbread from the South of England. You could say it is much more like parkin. It is best kept in an airtight tin for 2-3 days before eating.

INGREDIENTS

12oz	PLAIN FLOUR
1	ROUNDED TEASPOON GROUND GINGER
PINCH GRATED NUTMEG	
PINCH GROUND MIXED SPICE	
3oz	BUTTER (at room temperature)
8oz	BLACK TREACLE
1	TEASPOON BICARBONATE OF SODA
5	TABLESPOONS WARM MILK
1	LARGE EGG (beaten)

METHOD

PRE-HEAT OVEN 180ºC/350ºF/GAS 4

Grease and line a deep tin 10 inch x 8 inch.

Sift the flour and spices, then rub in the butter until it resembles fine breadcrumbs.

Warm the treacle gently.

Mix the bicarbonate of soda well into the warm milk and add to the treacle.

Make a well in the centre of the flour mixture.

Pour in the warm mixture together with the beaten egg.

Beat the mixture gently but thoroughly.

Pour into the prepared tin and cook in the oven for 30-40 minutes.

Leave to cool in the tin for 5 minutes before turning out on to a wire tray.

MAG'S COMMENT:
I DECIDED, FOR THAT EXTRA SPECIAL TREAT, TO DECORATE THE GINGERBREAD WITH A GINGER ICING, DECORATED WITH CHOPPED GLACE´ CRYSTALLISED GINGER
See page 152

BEST LEFT FOR ONE DAY BEFORE CUTTING

RICMOND MAIDS OF HONOUR

One traditional story tells us that one day during a stroll through Hampton Court, King Henry VIII came across a group of maids of honour – which included Anne Boleyn. The maids, attendants to the Queen, were eating cakes.

One of the cakes was offered to the King who tasted it and declared that it was delicious and wished to know its name. At the time, the mid 1520s, it had no name, so he decided that they should be called 'Maids of Honour.'

The cakes were the invention of the pastry cook to Catherine of Aragon, Henry's first wife, and for more than 200 years the recipe was a closely kept secret.

INGREDIENTS

8oz	PUFF PASTRY (see recipe on page 151) (If you are short of time, use ready made pastry)
8oz	CURD OR COTTAGE CHEESE
3oz	SUGAR
2oz	CURRANTS
	GRATED RIND OF 1 LEMON
½ oz	BLANCHED ALMONDS (chopped)
1	EGG (beaten)
2	TEASPOONS BRANDY
½oz	BUTTER (melted)

METHOD

PRE-HEAT OVEN 190°C/375°F/GAS 5

Rub the cheese through a fine sieve into a mixing bowl.

Add the sugar, currants, lemon rind, chopped almonds, egg, brandy and butter.

Mix well to combine the ingredients thoroughly.

Roll out the pastry and cut into rounds to line 16 greased patty tins.

Half fill the cases with the curd mixture.

Bake in the pre-heated oven for 20-30 minutes until golden brown.

Carefully transfer them to a wire cooling rack.

Don't be alarmed if they sink a little, that is normal.

SPRINKLE ON A LITTLE ICING SUGAR
BEFORE SERVING

RIPON CAKES

INGREDIENTS

3oz	BUTTER
3oz	GROUND ALMONDS
3oz	GROUND RICE
1	teaspoon ALMOND EXTRACT
3oz	CASTER SUGAR
4oz	SELF RAISING FLOUR
2	EGGS (beaten)
6	GLACE`CHERRIES (optional)

METHOD

PRE-HEAT OVEN 190ºC/375ºF/GAS 4

In a large bowl cream together the butter and sugar.

Beat in the eggs with a little of the flour and then fold in the remainder of the flour.

Fold in the almond extract, ground almonds and ground rice.

Turn into cake cases and place ½ cherry on top.

Bake in well greased bun tins or bun cases for approximately 15 – 20 minutes.

RIPON SPICE CAKE

A traditional loaf cake from North Yorkshire.
Here, fruit cake and wensleydale cheese
make a popular combination.
This recipe makes two loaves.

INGREDIENTS

10oz	SUGAR
8oz	BUTTER
3	EGGS (beaten)
2oz	MIXED PEEL
2oz	GLACE´ CHERRIES (chopped)
8oz	CURRANTS
8oz	RAISINS
1lb	PLAIN FLOUR
¼	PINT MILK
2oz	GROUND ALMONDS
2	TEASPOONS BAKING POWDER
2	TEASPOONS GROUND MIXED SPICE

METHOD

SERVE SLICED

PRE-HEAT OVEN 150ºC/300ºF/GAS 2

Cream together the butter and sugar until pale and fluffy.

Gradually add the eggs.

Toss the fruit in a little flour and stir into the mixture with the milk and ground almonds.

Add the remaining ingredients and fold into the mixture.

Divide the mixture between two greased and lined loaf tins and bake in the oven for approximately 1¾ hours.

When cold, store in an airtight container.

SCOTTISH PETTICOAT TAILS

These traditional Scottish shortbread biscuits date back before the 12th century. The triangles fit together into a circle and were the same shape as the pieces of fabric used to make a full-gored petticoat during the reign of Elizabeth I.

The name came from the word for the pattern which was 'tally', the biscuits became known as 'petticoat tails.'

INGREDIENTS

6oz BUTTER
3oz CASTER SUGAR (plus extra for dredging)
9oz PLAIN FLOUR

METHOD
PRE-HEAT OVEN 170°C/325°F/GAS 3

Grease and line a 7 inch sandwich tin.

Mix the flour and sugar in a bowl.

Rub in the butter.

Knead well to form a smooth paste.

Draw the mixture together and press into the lined sandwich tin.

Prick well all over.

Pinch up the edges with a finger and thumb.

Mark into 8 triangles.

Bake for approximately 40 minutes until a pale straw colour.

Leave in the tin for 5 minutes.

Cut into 8 triangles, then dredge with caster sugar.

REMOVE FROM THE TIN WHEN COLD
STORE IN AN AIRTIGHT CONTAINER

RICH SHORTBREAD THE TRADITIONAL
BRIDAL CAKE OF SCOTLAND

SCOTTISH SHORTBREAD

Shortbread is a mixture of flour, butter and sugar with other minor ingredients such as rice flour, marzipan, eggs, peel, almonds and walnuts added to make variations.

It is traditionally pressed into an embossed mould and released to reveal an attractive design on the top before baking.

A tradition with the shortbread was to break it over the head of the bride as she crossed the threshold of her new home. Thankfully the high butter content makes the shortbread very fragile and would not hurt those on the receiving end.

INGREDIENTS

8oz   BUTTER
4½ oz CASTER SUGAR
12oz   PLAIN FLOUR
CASTER SUGAR FOR SPRINKLING

SHORTBREAD KEEPS WELL IF STORED IN AN AIRTIGHT TIN

METHOD
PRE-HEAT OVEN 180°C/350°F/GAS 4

Rub the butter and sugar together, then work in the flour lightly with the fingertips. Continue mixing it until the ingredients form a dough.

Shape into a round ½ inch thick, or place inside a flan ring or press into a prepared mould.

Place on a lined baking sheet.

Prick all over with a fork, and mark across into segments.

Bake in the pre-heated oven for 40-45 minutes until light golden brown.

Allow the shortbread to cool a little before removing from the baking sheet.

Dust with caster sugar and leave on a wire rack until cold.

Alternatively, pat the dough into an oblong about ¼ inch thick and cut into shortbread fingers. Space out well on a greased baking sheet and bake in the pre-heated oven for 20-25 minutes.

SELKIRK BANNOCK

The Bannock is a flat loaf about the size of a dinner plate, traditionally baked on a griddle. The name derives from the latin panicum (bread).

In the past Bannocks were often made for special and festive occasions, for example, Christmas, the Bride's Bannock for May 1st and the Beltane Bannock baked on the first day of summer.

The Selkirk Bannock was first introduced in the mid-19th century by Robbie Douglas, who had a shop in Selkirk Top.

INGREDIENTS

THIS WILL MAKE THREE BANNOCKS

1lb SULTANAS
1lb STRONG WHITE FLOUR
1   LEVEL TEASPOON SALT
3oz BUTTER
3oz SUGAR
½   pint WARM MILK
1oz FRESH YEAST
A LITTLE BEATEN EGG TO GLAZE

METHOD

Soak the sultanas for 30 minutes in sufficient hot water to cover, then drain them and pat dry between pieces of kitchen paper.

Sieve the flour and salt into a large mixing bowl, rub in the butter and make a well in the centre.

Dissolve the sugar in the milk and use 3 tablespoons of this liquid to mix the yeast to a smooth paste.

Stir in the remaining milk and pour into the well.

Mix vigorously to blend, then knead for 5 minutes or more to make a smooth, springy dough. Use an electric mixer with a dough hook if you find this easier.

Shape the dough into a ball. Place in a warmed, lightly buttered bowl, cover with greased polythene and put in a warm place to rise for 30 minutes.

Gently knead in the sultanas without bursting them.

When they are well distributed throughout the dough, shape it into a ball again, cover with greased polythene and stand in a warm place to rise for a further 15 minutes.

Divide the dough into three equal pieces. Mould each into a smooth ball and place each on a warmed and lightly buttered baking sheet.

Cover with greased polythene and put in a warm place to rise for 1 hour, flattening the balls with the hand and brushing lightly with beaten egg after the first 15 minutes.

HEAT THE OVEN 215ºC/415ºF/GAS 6

Cook for about 20 minutes.

SHREWSBURY BISCUITS

Shrewsbury is a town with a long history and is famous for a particular type of biscuit. One of the better known recipes was by a Mr Palin, in 1819 , who was renowned for his particular mix. The original was very hard so modern recipes have been adapted to a softer version to cope with modern tastes.

The biscuits are light and lemony.

INGREDIENTS

4oz   BUTTER
5oz. CASTER SUGAR
2   EGG YOLKS
8oz   PLAIN FLOUR
1   LEMON (grated zest only)
2oz   CURRANTS OR RAISINS (optional)

METHOD
PRE-HEAT OVEN 180°C/350°F/GAS 4

Cream the butter and sugar together until pale and fluffy.

Add the egg yolks and beat well.

Stir in the flour and lemon zest, fruit, if required, and mix to a fairly firm dough.

Knead lightly on a floured surface and roll out to about ¼ inch thickness.

Cut out into ½ inch rounds with a fluted cutter, and put onto greased and lined baking sheets.

Bake for 15 minutes until lightly browned and firm to the touch.

TRANSFER TO WIRE RACKS TO COOL. STORE IN AN
AIRTIGHT CONTAINER TO RETAIN
THEIR CRISPNESS

SHROPSHIRE SOUL CAKES

On All Souls' Day, 2nd November, the dead are remembered and traditionally children would go 'a-souling'. They would sing 'a soul-cake, a soul-cake, please, good missus, a soul-cake. One for Peter, one for Paul, three for him who saved us all.' They would receive in return, a cake marked with a cross.

INGREDIENTS

6oz   BUTTER
6oz   CASTER SUGAR
3   EGG YOLKS
1lb   PLAIN FLOUR
PINCH OF SALT
1   TEASPOON GROUND MIXED SPICE
WARM MILK
(If desired a few threads of saffron can be soaked in the warm milk straining it before use.)

METHOD
PRE-HEAT OVEN 180°C/350°F/GAS 4

Cream the butter and sugar together in a bowl until fluffy.

Beat in the egg yolks.

Sift together the flour, salt and spice.

Fold into the egg mixture with the currants, adding sufficient milk to form a soft dough.

Turned the mixture on to a lightly floured surface.

Press the mixture down lightly to about ¼ inch thickness.

Cut the cakes with a plain cutter before flattening a little.

Mark with a cross.

Place on a greased and lined baking sheet and bake for 15-20 minutes or until golden in colour.

SNOWDON PUDDING

This white-capped pudding was named in honour of the legend - Haunted Yr Wyddfa – Snowdon – on whose summit, the highest in Wales, snow often lies until late spring.

INGREDIENTS

4oz	STONED RAISINS
8oz	SHREDDED SUET
1½oz	PLAIN FLOUR OR CORNFLOUR
6oz	BROWN SUGAR (I used soft dark brown sugar)
8oz	WHITE BREADCRUMBS
6oz	LEMON MARMALADE

GRATED RIND OF 2 LEMONS

¼	TEASPOON SALT
6	EGGS (beaten)

METHOD

POUR OVER THE SAUCE JUST BEFORE TAKING IT TO THE TABLE

Put aside about 1 tablespoon of the raisins, then mix the rest together with the suet, flour, brown sugar, breadcrumbs, marmalade, grated lemon rind and salt.

Beat the eggs and stir into the mixture.

Sprinkle the tablespoon raisins over the bottom of a 3 pint greased basin and pour the pudding mixture on top of them.

Prepare the pudding for steaming, cover with a lid and boil for 3 hours, topping up with boiling water from time to time to maintain the level.

TO MAKE THE SAUCE

INGREDIENTS

1½oz	CASTER SUGAR

RIND OF ½ LEMON

¼	PINT WATER
1oz	BUTTER
2	LEVEL TEASPOONS PLAIN FLOUR OR CORNFLOUR
4floz	WHITE WINE

METHOD

Boil the sugar and lemon rind in the ¼ pint of water for about 15 minutes, then discard the rind and add the butter.

Take the pan off the heat and cool it for 10-15 minutes, then stir in the flour to make a smooth mixture.

Work in the wine, return the pan to the stove and stir over a gentle heat until the sauce thickens.

Serve the pudding piping hot.

SOMERSET APPLE CAKE

Both Somerset and Dorset lay claim to this deliciously moist cake which is equally good served with cream and eaten warm as a pudding.

The cake is best consumed within two days of being made.

INGREDIENTS

4oz	BUTTER
6oz	DARK SOFT BROWN SUGAR
2	EGGS (beaten)
8oz	PLAIN FLOUR
1	TEASPOON GROUND MIXED SPICE
1	TEASPOON GROUND CINNAMON
2	TEASPOON BAKING POWDER
1lb	COOKING APPLES (peeled, cored and chopped)
3-4	TABLESPOONS MILK
1	TABLESPOON CLEAR HONEY
1	TABLESPOON DEMERARA SUGAR

METHOD

PRE-HEAT OVEN 170°C/325°F/GAS 3

Grease and line a deep 7 inch round cake tin with greaseproof paper.

Cream the butter and sugar together in a bowl until pale and fluffy.

Gradually add the eggs, beating well after each addition.

Add the flour, spices, baking powder and mix well.

Fold in the apples and enough milk to give a soft dropping consistency.

Turn into the prepared tin and bake for 1½ hours until well risen and firm to the touch.

Turn onto a wire rack to cool completely.

WHEN COLD, BRUSH THE TOP
WITH HONEY
AND SPRINKLE WITH DEMERARA
SUGAR TO DECORATE

STAFFORDSHIRE FRUIT CAKE

A rich fruit cake, which has the addition of black treacle and brandy.

INGREDIENTS

6 oz BUTTER
6oz SOFT BROWN SUGAR
4 EGGS
8oz PLAIN FLOUR
½ TEASPOON GROUND MACE
½ TEASPOON BAKING POWDER
2oz BLACK TREACLE
2oz GROUND ALMONDS
8oz CURRANTS
2oz GLACE´ CHERRIES, QUARTERED
2oz MIXED PEEL
1 TABLESPOON BRANDY
2 TEASPOON LEMON JUICE

METHOD

PRE-HEAT OVEN
180°C/350°F/GAS 4

Grease and line an 8 inch round cake tin.

Cream the butter and sugar together in a bowl until light and fluffy.

Whisk the eggs together in a bowl set over a pan of hot water then beat into the butter mixture.

Stir together the flour, mace and baking powder. Fold into the butter mixture, alternately with the treacle and ground almonds.

Mix the currants, cherries and peel together and stir into the mixture with the brandy and lemon juice.

Turn the mixture into the prepared tin and smooth over the top.

Bake for 2 hours, covering the top with a piece of kitchen foil or grease proof paper if it appears to be browning too quickly.

Allow to cool in the tin for 5 minutes, then turn out on to a wire rack to continue cooling.

SUFFOLK GOOSEBERRY CUSTARD

This very old recipe is a forerunner of the more modern gooseberry fool. 'Custard' was the usual Suffolk description of a creamy dessert or pudding.

INGREDIENTS

1lb	GOOSEBERRIES (topped and tailed)
¼	PINT WATER
½oz	BUTTER
½	TABLESPOON ROSEWATER OR LEMON JUICE
4oz	SUGAR
¼	PINT DOUBLE CREAM
2	EGGS

METHOD

Wash the gooseberries and drain well.

Put in a saucepan with the water and simmer until soft.

Mash gently with a fork before stirring in the butter, rosewater or lemon juice and sugar.

Cook gently until the sugar is completely dissolved.

Whisk the cream and eggs together, then stir into the gooseberry mixture.

Cook over a low heat, stirring, until thickened.

Pour into a serving bowl and chill.

Serve with small, sweet biscuits.

SUFFOLK RAISIN ROLY-POLY

INGREDIENTS

6oz RAISINS
4oz SUET
3oz SELF RAISING FLOUR
2   TEASPOONS SOFT BROWN SUGAR
1   TEASPOON BAKING POWDER
PINCH OF SALT
GRANULATED SUGAR FOR SPRINKLING

METHOD

Mix the flour, salt and baking powder together.

Add the suet, 2oz of the raisins, and enough cold water to form a soft dough.

Turn out on to a lightly floured surface and roll into an oblong about 1/4 inch thick.

Sprinkle the remainder of the raisins and the sugar on to the dough, then roll up like a swiss roll, dampening the ends and pressing firmly together to seal.

Sprinkle with a little flour, then wrap lightly in greaseproof paper. Roll up in a lightly floured pudding cloth, tying the ends tightly.

Place in a saucepan of boiling water and boil for 2 hours, topping up the water as necessary.

Serve cut into thick slices, sprinkled with granulated sugar with custard or cream.

Delicious served with custard, cream or ice cream.

SUSSEX POND PUDDING

The name of this suet pudding is derived from the moat of buttery sauce that surrounds it. The inclusion of a whole lemon adds a brilliant piquancy to the sugar and butter sauce.

INGREDIENTS

8oz	SUET CRUST PASTRY
4oz	BUTTER, CUT INTO SMALL FLAKES
4oz	DEMERARA SUGAR
1	LARGE LEMON
	Washed and pricked all over with a thin skewer

METHOD

Roll out the suet crust pastry into a large circle on a floured board.

With a sharp knife, cut out a quarter segment of the circle and keep this to use as a lid.

Put the remaining pastry into a greased 1½ pint basin to line it.

Dampen the cuts and press to seal.

Pack half the butter flakes and half the sugar into the suet crust lining and set the whole lemon on top.

Cover with the remaining flaked butter and sugar.

Roll out the reserved quarter of pastry into a circle, and put on top of the pudding. Press the edges to seal them.

Prepare the basin for steaming and steam in a covered saucepan for 3½ hours, adding more boiling water as necessary to maintain the level.

Turn the pudding out carefully on to a hot shallow dish and serve hot with custard, cream or lemon sauce.

**MAKE SURE WHEN SERVING
THE PUDDING THAT EVERYONE
RECEIVES A SMALL PIECE OF
LEMON ON THEIR PLATE**

SUTTON PIE

This apple recipe originates from Sutton in Surrey. The recipe is unusual in that it uses porridge oats for a topping.

INGREDIENTS

5oz   BUTTER

1 lb   COOKING APPLES, PEELED, CORED AND SLICED

JUICE AND GRATED ZEST OF ½ SMALL LEMON

2-3   TABLESPOONS ORANGE MARMALADE

8oz   SELF RAISING FLOUR

3oz   SOFT LIGHT BROWN SUGAR

3oz   PORRIDGE OATS

METHOD

PRE-HEAT OVEN 190°C/375°F/GAS 5

Place the apples, lemon zest, juice and 1/2oz of the butter in a saucepan. Add a little water, if necessary, and cook the apples until soft.

Sieve to form a puree and stir in the marmalade.

Combine the flour and remaining butter until the mixture resembles fine breadcrumbs then stir in the sugar and the oats.

Melt a very little butter in a frying pan and cook the oat mixture over a low heat for about one minute, stirring continuously.

Butter a shallow 7-8 inch flan dish.

Divide the oat mixture in half and press one half on to the base of the flan dish.

Spread on the apple mixture and top with the remaining oat mixture.

Sprinkle a little extra brown sugar over the flan and dot with butter.

Cook for 40-50 minutes.

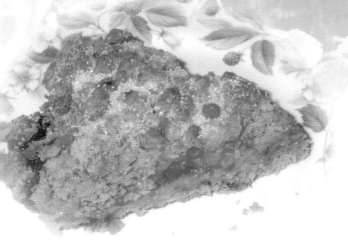

SERVE WITH CUSTARD, CREAM OR ICE-CREAM

WAKEFIELD GINGERBREAD

INGREDIENTS

5oz	BUTTER
11oz	SELF RAISING FLOUR
5oz	CASTER SUGAR
1½oz	CHOPPED MIXED PEEL
2	TEASPOONS GROUND GINGER
4oz	GOLDEN SYRUP
1	DESSERTSPOON BRANDY

**TWO WAKEFIELD LADIES
ENJOYING THEIR GINGERBREAD**

METHOD
PRE-HEAT OVEN 180ºC/350ºF/GAS 4

Grease and line an 8 inch square shallow cake tin or equivalent.

Sift the flour into a bowl and rub in the butter until the mixture resembles breadcrumbs.

Add the sugar, ground ginger and mixed peel. Stir together.

Warm the syrup with the brandy in a pan over a low heat and then add to the mixture in the bowl and work in well to a soft consistency.

Spoon into the tin and bake for 1½ - 2 hours or until a skewer inserted comes out clean.

Transfer to a wire rack and cut into squares when cold.

WALSINGHAM HONEY CAKE

Walsingham has long been famous for its bees and the quality of their honey.
This cake betrays its medieval origins with a mixture of honey, treacle and ginger.

INGREDIENTS

8oz	BUTTER
8oz	LIGHT SOFT BROWN SUGAR
½	PINT MILK
3oz	BLACK TREACLE
3oz	CLEAR HONEY
2	EGGS
1lb	PLAIN FLOUR
1	TEASPOON GROUND GINGER
1	TEASPOON BICARBONATE OF SODA
4oz	SEEDLESS RAISINS
2oz	CHOPPED MIXED PEEL
2oz	GLACE´ CHERRIES (cut into quarters)

FOR THE TOPPING

4	TABLESPOONS CLEAR HONEY
1½oz	SOFT LIGHT BROWN SUGAR
2oz	BUTTER
2oz	FLAKED ALMONDS

METHOD

PRE-HEAT OVEN 160ºC/325ºF/GAS 3

Grease and line an 8 inch square cake tin.

Cream the butter and sugar until light and fluffy.

Put the milk, treacle and honey into a pan and heat to lukewarm.

Beat into the creamed mixture with the eggs.

Sieve the flour, ginger and soda together and beat into the mixture.

Stir in the raisins, peel and cherries.

Put into the prepared tin and bake
for 2 – 2 ¼ hours, until firm.

TO MAKE THE TOPPING

Warm the honey, sugar and
butter together until just melted.

Spread on the warm cake and
sprinkle with almonds.

Leave the cake until cold
before removing from the tin.

WARWICK PUDDING

INGREDIENTS

4	TABLESPOONS GINGER WINE
2oz	DRIED FIGS (trimmed and finely chopped)
½	PINT MILK
3	EGG YOLKS
2oz	CASTER SUGAR
1oz	GELATINE
4	TABLESPOONS WATER
½	PINT DOUBLE CREAM
1oz	PRESERVED GINGER (very finely chopped)

WHIPPED CREAM FOR DECORATION

METHOD

Soak the chopped figs in ginger wine overnight.

Drain off the wine from the figs and set both aside.

Put the milk into a saucepan and heat until almost boiling.

Whisk the egg yolks and sugar together and stir into the milk, combining well.

Stir gently over a low heat until the custard is creamy, then allow to cool.

Put the gelatine in a cup with the water and stand in a saucepan of hot water, stirring gently until the gelatine has dissolved and is syrupy.

Stir the melted gelatine into the ginger wine and set aside until lukewarm.

Whip the cream until it stands in soft peaks.

Stir the gelatine into the custard, then combine together the custard and the cream, whisking well.

Leave to cool and thicken, then stir in the chopped ginger.

Add the drained figs, stir lightly, pour into a glass serving bowl and leave to set.

Decorate with whipped cream and serve with pouring cream.

WELSH AMBER PUDDING

A rich tart with an orange and lemon flavour.

INGREDIENTS

8oz SHORTCRUST PASTRY
4oz BUTTER
2oz CASTER SUGAR
2   EGGS
2   EGG YOLKS
GRATED ZEST OF HALF A LEMON
2   TABLESPOONS MARMALADE

METHOD

PRE-HEAT OVEN220ºC/425ºF/GAS 7

Roll out the pastry on a floured surface.

Line a greased 7 inch round baking tin with pastry.

Prick the pastry base with a fork. Cover with a layer of greaseproof paper and some baking beans.

Bake for 10-12 minutes, until the pastry is quite firm but not coloured.

Reduce the heat to 190ºC 375ºF/Gas 5.

Melt the butter.

Whisk the eggs, yolks, sugar, lemon zest and marmalade together.

Whisk in the melted butter.

Pour into the prepared pastry case.

Bake for 20-25 minutes or until set.

Delicious served hot, warm or cold.

WELSH BARA BRITH

Words Bara Brith mean 'speckled.' Bread was originally made for special occasions such as harvest, Easter and Christmas.

This North Wales speciality has a rich, fruity mixture under a firm nutty crust.

INGREDIENTS

10oz	STRONG WHITE FLOUR
1	LEVEL TEASPOON SALT
¾oz	LARD
1oz	SUGAR
½	LEVEL TEASPOON GROUND MIXED SPICE
1	LARGE EGG (beaten)
¼	PINT WARM WATER
¾oz	FRESH YEAST
8oz	CURRANTS
4oz	SULTANAS
1oz	CHOPPED, MIXED DRIED PEEL

METHOD

Sieve the flour and salt into a large mixing bowl.

Rub in the lard and make a well in the centre.

Mix the sugar and spice together and put into the well.

Combine the beaten egg with the warm water and use 3 tablespoons of it to mix the yeast to a smooth, thin paste, then stir in the rest of the liquid.

Pour over the sugar in the well, mix vigorously to blend. Knead well to make a smooth, elastic dough- if you prefer use a dough hook in an electric mixer.

Mix together the currants, sultanas, peel and knead lightly into the dough.

Mould the dough into a round or long shape and put on a greased baking sheet, or in a greased 2lb loaf tin.

Cover with greased polythene and put in a warm place to rise.

HEAT OVEN 180ºC/350ºF/GAS 4

Bake for approximately 35 minutes until dark golden brown on top.

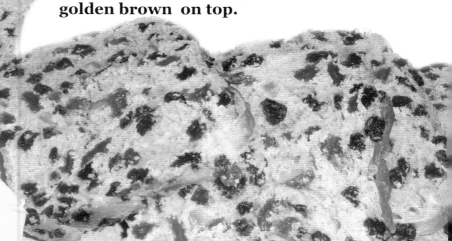

WELSH CINNAMON CAKE

INGREDIENTS

4oz BUTTER
4oz CASTER SUGAR
2   EGG YOLKS
8oz SELF RAISING FLOUR
½   TEASPOON BAKING POWDER
1   ROUNDED TEASPOON
      CINNAMON
APRICOT JAM
3   EGG WHITES
3   TABLESPOONS CASTER SUGAR

METHOD

PRE-HEAT OVEN 200°C/400°F/GAS 5

In a large bowl, cream together the butter and caster sugar.

Beat in the egg yolks.

Sift the flour, baking powder and cinnamon together.

Mix into the butter mixture.

Knead to a dough and roll out to fit into an 8½ inch tart tin, with a removable base.

Bake for 20 minutes.

Cool the cake on a wire rack after removing it from the tin.

Heat a good tablespoon of apricot jam with a little water. Sieve it and brush thinly over the cake.

Beat the egg whites until they are stiff.

Fold in the caster sugar.

Pile on to the cake, swirling the top into decorative points.

Bake again reducing heat to 180°C/350°F/GAS 4
until the meringue is golden and set – about 15 minutes.

WELSH RASPBERRY GRIDDLE SCONES

The name 'scone' is believed to come from the Gaelic word Sgonn, or 'large mouthful.'

Raspberries are a truly native fruit and the wild variety was eaten by the bronze age inhabitants of Britain.

They were recorded in Britain as a garden fruit until the 16th century – but they had probably been cultivated for some time before that.

It was the Welsh who first used raspberries in combination with griddle scones. The result was a favourite dish in medieval times.

INGREDIENTS

4oz   SELF RAISING FLOUR
¼   TEASPOON SALT
½   TEASPOON BAKING POWDER OR
BICARBONATE OF SODA
1   EGG (beaten)
½   PINT SOUR MILK (approximately)
4-6oz RASPBERRIES
CASTER SUGAR FOR SPRINKLING
(Sour milk makes the scones lighter.
If you have none, add a little vinegar
to fresh milk until it curdles.)

MAG'S COMMENT:
I HAVE ALSO USED STRAWBERRIES
AND APRICOTS IN THIS RECIPE
BOTH EQUALLY DELICIOUS

SPRINKLE WITH SUGAR - SERVE HOT OR COLD

METHOD

Sift together the flour, salt and baking powder.

Make a well in the centre and pour in the egg and half the milk.

Beat well, adding more milk as necessary, to form a batter the consistency of thick cream.

Stir in the fruit.

Heat the griddle or heavy-based frying pan and smear with a little butter or lard.

Drop 3-4 separate tablespoons of the batter mixture on to it, spacing them out well to allow them to spread without running together.

Cook for about 1½ minutes or until bubbles appear.

Turn over and cook the second side a little, taking care not to burn the fruit.

Lift the scones on to a plate, using a palette knife.

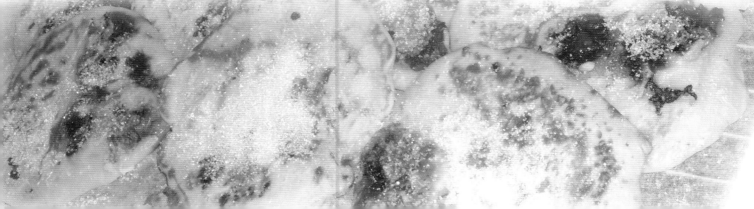

WELSH TEISEN LAP

This moist cake was popular with miners who ate it down the mines in the South Wales Valleys.

Traditionally the cake would have been made in a shallow tin and cooked in front of an open fire.

INGREDIENTS

8oz PLAIN FLOUR
1   PINCH OF SALT
1   TEASPOON BAKING POWDER
1   PINCH NUTMEG
4oz BUTTER
2oz CASTER SUGAR
4oz CURRANTS
2   EGGS (well beaten)
¼   PINT MILK (approx)

MAG'S COMMENT:
I PREFER TO USE
SULTANAS OR RAISINS IN THIS RECIPE

METHOD

PRE-HEAT OVEN 180ºC/350ºF/GAS 4

Grease and line a shallow 7 inch square baking tin.

Sieve the flour, salt, baking powder and nutmeg into a bowl.   Rub in the butter. Add the sugar and fruit.

Beat the eggs well and mix into the dry ingredients.

Add the milk slowly and beat well to make a soft dough.

Pour the mixture into the tin and bake for 30-40 minutes until light golden brown.

WESTMORLAND PEPPER CAKE

If you are unfamiliar with using pepper in recipes you will be pleasantly surprised by its effect. It adds unusual spiciness to what is otherwise a fairly standard fruit cake.

It is just one example of the huge variety of fruit cake recipes from this part of the world.

INGREDIENTS

3oz RAISINS
3oz CURRANTS
4oz CASTER SUGAR
3oz BUTTER
¼   PINT WATER
8oz SELF RAISING FLOUR
½   TEASPOON GROUND GINGER
LARGE PINCH GROUND CLOVES
½   TEASPOON FINELY
      GROUND BLACK PEPPER
4   TABLESPOONS MILK
1   EGG (beaten)

METHOD

PRE-HEAT OVEN 350°F/180°C/GAS 4

Grease and line a 7 inch cake tin.

Put the fruit, sugar, butter and water in a saucepan and bring slowly to the boil.

Leave to cool slightly.

Put the flour, spices and pepper in a bowl and gently stir in the fruit mixture, milk, and the egg

Mix thoroughly without beating.

Turn the mixture into the prepared tin and bake for about 50 minutes or until firm to the touch and golden brown.

TURN OUT AND LEAVE TO COOL ON A WIRE RACK

WESTMORLAND RUM CAKE

INGREDIENTS

8oz	RAISINS
8oz	CURRANTS
8oz	DATES (chopped)
3oz	GLACE` CHERRIES (sliced)
10floz	RUM
5floz	SHERRY
8oz	BUTTER
12oz	SELF RAISING FLOUR
1	TEASPOON BICARBONATE OF SODA
4	EGGS
½	TEASPOON MIXED SPICE
½	TEASPOON CINNAMON
¼	TEASPOON NUTMEG
8oz	DARK SOFT BROWN SUGAR

METHOD

In a large bowl place the raisins, currants, dates and cherries.

Pour the rum and sherry over the fruit.

Leave to soak for three days.

Into a large bowl sift the flour with the bicrabonate of soda, and all the spices.

In another bowl cream the butter and the sugar until creamy in texture.

Beat in the eggs one at a time and add to the creamed mixture, alternately with the flour.

Next stir in all the fruit mixture.
Spoon the cake into a greased and lined 8 inch cake tin.

PRE-HEAT OVEN 350°F/180°C/GAS 4

Hollow out the top of the cake so that it will rise evenly.

Wrap a layer of brown paper around the outside of the tin.

Bake for 2-2 ½ hours in the centre of the oven.

When the cake is cold wrap in foil.

BEST IF KEPT FOR AT LEAST TWO WEEKS BEFORE CUTTING

WESTMORLAND SPICE CAKE

INGREDIENTS

3	EGGS
6oz	CASTER SUGAR
10floz	CLEAR HONEY
4oz	CHOPPED ALMONDS
	GRATED RIND OF ½ ORANGE
	GRATED RIND OF ½ LEMON
2oz	MIXED PEEL
10oz	SELF RAISING FLOUR
¼	TEASPOON GROUND CLOVES
¼	TEASPOON GRATED NUTMEG
½	TEASPOON GROUND CINNAMON

METHOD

PRE-HEAT OVEN 350°F/180°C/GAS 4

In a large mixing bowl, beat the eggs and sugar until pale and fluffy.

Stir in the honey, almonds, mixed peel, lemon and orange rind.

Stir in the flour and all the spices.

Continue stirring until thoroughly mixed.

Pour the mixture into a greased and lined 8 inch square cake tin.

Wrap a layer of brown paper around the outside of the tin.

Place in the centre of the oven and bake for 50-60 minutes.

THIS CAKE CAN BE ICED OR SIMPLY SERVED
SLICED AND SPREAD WITH BUTTER

WESTMORLAND THREE DECKER

INGREDIENTS

1lb   COOKING APPLES
      (peeled, cored and chopped)
3   TABLESPOONS SUGAR
A LITTLE MILK FOR COATING
1   TABLESPOON DEMARARA
      SUGAR FOR SPRINKLING

FOR THE PASTRY
6oz PLAIN FLOUR
3oz BUTTER
WATER FOR MIXING

METHOD

Line a 6 inch cake tin with foil.

PRE-HEAT OVEN 375°F/190°C/GAS 4

In a large mixing bowl, rub the butter into the flour and add just enough cold water to make a soft dough.

Knead lightly on a floured surface.

Roll out the pastry and cut four circles using the base of the tin as a guide.

Put a circle of pastry in the bottom of the tin and cover with a third of the fruit and sugar.

Repeat twice, then put the final circle of pastry on top.

Brush the top with milk and sprinkle with 1 tablespoon of demerara sugar.

Bake in the oven for 20 minutes then turn down the oven to 180°c/350°f for a further 30 minutes, or until the filling is cooked.

WILTSHIRE LARDY CAKE

Traditionally Wiltshire was an area that went in for pig rearing in a big way and developed tasty dishes to use up every scrap of the animal.

The lardy cake relates back to the 'Old English Fair' which was an eagerly awaited event by town and countrymen who would get together to sell their wares. Essentially a country bread, lardy cake has been called 'the countryman's answer to a fruit cake', being an adapted version of the plum cake. This cake was once baked to celebrate the harvest. In the West Country bakers still make lardy cake to their own recipes, using as much lard, sugar and fruit as they choose.

INGREDIENTS

THIS WILL MAKE TWO LOAVES

1lb   STRONG WHITE FLOUR
1   LEVEL TEASPOON SALT
1oz   LARD
2oz   SUGAR
1oz   FRESH YEAST
½   PINT WARM MILK
8oz   CURRANTS
4oz   SULTANAS

FOR THE FILLING
4oz   LARD
4oz   SOFT BROWN SUGAR
1   TEASPOON GROUND MIXED SPICE

METHOD

Sieve the flour and salt into a large mixing bowl.

Rub in the lard and make a well in the centre of the mixture.

Mix the sugar and yeast in a jug to a smooth, thin paste with three tablespoons of the warm milk.

Stir in the rest of the milk and pour into the well.

Mix vigorously to make a smooth dough.

Shape into a ball and put in a large greased bowl.

Cover with greased polythene and stand in a warm place to rise for 30 minutes.

Lightly knead the currants and sultanas into the dough, then let it rest, covered for 10 minutes before rolling out into a long rectangle 18in x 6in.

Make the filling by mixing together the lard, brown sugar and ground mixed spice, and then spread it along two-thirds of the rolled dough.

Fold the unspread one-third over the centre section and then the remaining spread section over these.

Roll out the dough again to the same size as before.

Roll it up from a short side like a swiss roll.

Cut the roll in half to give two rolled pieces 3in long.

Stand each piece, cut end uppermost, in a lined round tin 6in across.

Cover with greased polythene and stand in a warm place to rise for 40 minutes.

PRE-HEAT OVEN 400°F/200°C/GAS 6

Bake in the oven for 30 minutes.

CAUTION – HANDLE WITH A THICK CLOTH AS IT WILL BE EXTREMELY HOT

Turn out of the tins immediately to let the hot filling run over the loaves and form a glaze.

YORK BISCUITS

INGREDIENTS

4oz   PLAIN FLOUR
4oz   LIGHT BROWN SUGAR
2oz   LARD OR MARGARINE
2   LEVEL TEASPOONS
GROUND GINGER
1   SMALL EGG
1   LEVEL TEASPOON CREAM
       OF TARTAR
½   LEVEL TEASPOON
BICARBONATE OF SODA
MILK AS REQUIRED

METHOD
PRE-HEAT OVEN 180ºC/350ºF/GAS 4

Cream in a basin together the lard or margarine and the sugar.

Add the egg.

Sift the dry ingredients and work into the mixture, adding the milk as necessary. (The consistency should not be too soft, but not stiff.)

Divide the mixture into 16 round balls.

Place onto greased and lined baking trays, flattening them slightly.

Bake for approximately 20 minutes or until lightly browned.

Turn out on to a wire rack to cool.

YORKSHIRE CHEESE CAKES

These small cheesecakes are traditionally baked in Ripon in the first week of August to commemorate St Wilfrid, the town's Patron Saint.

INGREDIENTS

8oz SHORTCRUST PASTRY
½   PINT MILK
10z FRESH WHITE BREADCRUMBS
4oz BUTTER
2oz GROUND ALMONDS
10z CASTER SUGAR
GRATED RIND OF 1 LEMON
3   EGGS

METHOD
PRE-HEAT OVEN 180ºC/350ºF/GAS 4

Grease about 20 patty tins.

Roll out the pastry on a lightly floured surface.

Cut out circles and line the patty tins.

Pour the milk into a saucepan, bring to the boil and stir in the breadcrumbs.

Leave to stand for about 10 minutes, then add the butter, ground almonds, sugar and lemon rind to the milk mixture.

Beat in the eggs, one at a time.

Spoon the mixture into each patty case and bake for 20-25 minutes until set.

Turn out on to a wire rack to cool.

ENJOY WITH A NICE CUP OF TEA OR AS A LIGHT
PUDDING, SERVED WITH CREAM

YORKSHIRE FAT RASCALS

Fat Rascals are round domed teacakes
with a rich brown crust made with
currants and candied peel.

The origin of the name is unknown,
but has been in use since at least the
Mid-Nineteenth Century.

INGREDIENTS

2oz	LARD
2oz	BUTTER
12oz	PLAIN FLOUR
3oz	CURRANTS
1oz	CANDIED MIXED PEEL
1	HEAPED TEASPOON BAKING POWDER
3oz	CASTER SUGAR
5floz	WHIPPING CREAM (slightly soured)

METHOD

PRE-HEAT OVEN 220ºC/425ºF/GAS 7

In a large mixing bowl, rub the butter and lard into
the flour until it resembles fine breadcrumbs.

Add the sugar and the dry ingredients.

Pour in the cream and mix to a stiff paste.

On a lightly floured board, roll the mixture
out to ¾ inch thickness and cut into rounds.
(This recipe should make about ten teacakes.)

Place on a lined baking sheet.

Bake in the oven for approximately 10-15 minutes.

DELICIOUS EATEN STRAIGHT
FROM THE THE OVEN

MR 'GINGER' BACON

144

YORKSHIRE PARKIN

It has long been the tradition to eat Parkin around the bonfire, on 5th November, Guy Fawkes' Night. The recipe is associated with the winter months. The recipe developed because of the plentiful supply of oats. The farmhouse oven was ideal for baking Parkin once it had cooled slightly after the bread making.

The connection with the Gunpowder Plot conspirator is that he was a Yorkshire man, born in York in 1570.

The dark cake is sometimes eaten with a topping of stewed apple or accompanied by cheese. It is best kept in an airtight tin. It is said that in Georgian times parkin and gingerbreads were stored in a special wooden container.

INGREDIENTS

4oz	SELF RAISING FLOUR
1	TEASPOON GROUND GINGER
1	TEASPOON BICARBONATE OF SODA
¼	TEASPOON SALT
4oz	FINE OATMEAL
1oz	CHOPPED MIXED PEEL
4oz	BLACK TREACLE
2oz	SOFT BROWN SUGAR
2oz	BUTTER OR MARGARINE
1	EGG, BEATEN
2	TABLESPOONS MILK

METHOD
PRE-HEAT OVEN 170°C/325°F/GAS 3

Sift together in a bowl the flour, ginger, bicarbonate of soda and salt.

Mix in the oatmeal and then the peel.

Melt the treacle, sugar and butter together, gently.

Stir in the egg with a wooden spoon.

Pour the mixture over the dry ingredients.

Mix well and add enough of the milk to make a soft, pouring consistency.

Pour into a well-greased and lined shallow tin, 6 inches square, and bake for about one hour, or until firm in the centre.

Cut into squares when the cake has cooled.

IF YOU WISH, SUBSTITUTE THE BLACK TREACLE WITH GOLDEN SYRUP. THIS RESULTS IN THE CAKE BEING LIGHTER IN COLOUR AND FLAVOUR

YORKSHIRE RHUBARB GINGERBREAD

This gingerbread incorporates a layer of chopped rhubarb and crystallised ginger through the centre.

INGREDIENTS

4oz	BUTTER
2oz	CASTER SUGAR
1½oz	BLACK TREACLE
4oz	SELF RAISING FLOUR
½	TEASPOON BICARBONATE OF SODA
3	TEASPOONS GROUND GINGER
1	EGG (beaten)
MILK TO MIX	
1¼lb	RHUBARB (chopped into pieces)
6oz	CRYSTALLISED GINGER (chopped)

METHOD

PRE-HEAT OVEN 180ºC/350ºF/GAS 4

Grease and line an 6 inch square shallow cake tin.

Melt the butter, sugar and treacle together in a pan over a low heat.

Remove from the heat.

Sift together the flour, bicarbonate of soda and 1 teaspoon of the ground ginger.

Stir into the mixture in the pan.

Stir in the beaten egg and enough milk, if required, to give a soft consistency.

Spoon half the mixture into the tin, top evenly with the rhubarb pieces and crystallised ginger and sprinkle over the remaining 2 teaspoons ground ginger.

Spoon over the remaining gingerbread mixture and smooth out.

Bake for about 1 ½ hours or until a skewer inserted comes out clean.

Turn out on to a wire rack and cut into squares when cold.

MAG'S COMMENT:
THIS IS ONE OF THE MOST FASCINATING RECIPES I'VE EVER MADE. I WAS QUITE CONVINCED IT WOULDN'T WORK. THANK GOODNESS I WAS WRONG. FOR THE LOVERS OF GINGER, YOU MUST TRY IT.
DELICIOUS AS A HOT SWEET SERVED WITH CUSTARD OR POURING CREAM.

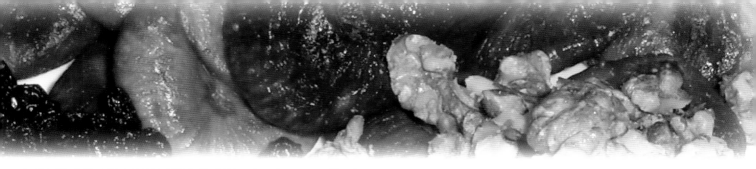

YORKSHIRE SLY CAKES

Sometimes known as 'sally sly cakes' these are among our earliest party treats. These were traditionally Cornish cakes containing currants and candied peel.

The recipe dates from the beginning of the 16th century. They probably got their name from their surprise element, for lying beneath their plain golden brown tops is a rich filling of figs, raisins, currants and nuts.

INGREDIENTS

1 lb   SHORTCRUST PASTRY (with 2oz sugar added with the fat)
A LITTLE MILK TO GLAZE
6oz   DRIED FIGS (chopped)
2oz   RAISINS
2oz   CURRANTS
2oz   CHOPPED WALNUTS
2oz   SUGAR
4   TABLESPOONS WATER

METHOD

PRE-HEAT OVEN 190ºC/375ºF/GAS 5

To make the filling, put the figs in a pan with the raisins, currants, walnuts and sugar.

Add the water and simmer until the figs are tender and the water has been absorbed.

Leave to cool.

Roll out half the pastry to line a greased, shallow oblong tin, about 9 inch x 4 inch.

Spread on the filling and dampen the rim of the pastry with water.

Roll out the remaining pastry, lay it over the filling and pinch the edges together to seal.

Brush with milk and bake in a pre-heated oven for 25-30 minutes, or until golden brown.

Sprinkle with sugar and cut into squares when cool.

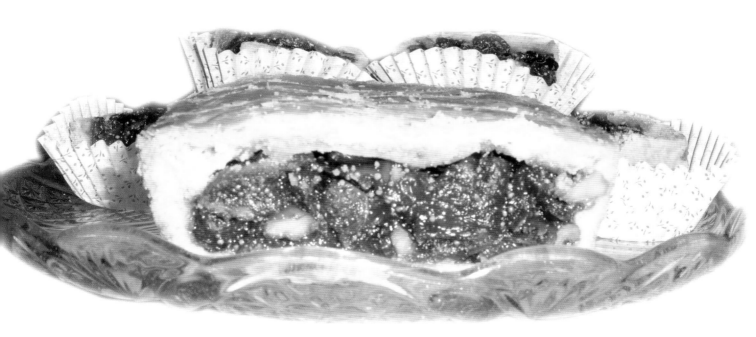

YORKSHIRE TEACAKES

INGREDIENTS

2oz	CURRANTS
2oz	SULTANAS
1 lb	STRONG WHITE FLOUR
1	LEVEL TEASPOON SALT
1½oz	LARD
2oz	SUGAR
½	PINT WARM MILK
1oz	FRESH YEAST

METHOD
PRE-HEAT OVEN 225°C/450°F/GAS 6

Rinse the currants and sultanas with warm water, pat dry with kitchen paper and leave in a warm place.

Sieve the flour and salt into a large mixing bowl, rub in the lard and make a well in the centre.

Dissolve the sugar in the milk and use 3 tablespoons of the liquid to mix the yeast to a smooth paste.

Stir in the rest of the milk and pour the liquid into the well.

Mix thoroughly to blend well and then knead until the mixture forms a smooth, elastic dough.

Work in the currants and sultanas.

Shape the dough into a ball, put it into a warm, greased bowl, cover and leave in a warm place to rise for about 45 minutes.

Turn the dough on to a lightly floured working surface and knead for a few minutes to a smooth, even texture.

Reshape it into a ball, cover again and put to rise for 15 minutes.

Divide the dough into 12 pieces. Shape each piece into a smooth ball. With a rolling pin, roll out the dough balls into 3 ½ inch discs. Place them on baking sheets.

Cover with greased polythene and set to rise in a warm place for approximately 40 minutes.

Teacakes are said to be direct descendants of Manchet or 'Handbread' – a medieval loaf in which fine flour was used, and the loaf shaped by hand and cooked without a tin.

There are two versions of the teacake – fruit or plain. The fruited teacake was originally a Lenten speciality. They are served split and buttered or toasted and buttered. These large, flat buns are particularly enjoyable on a cold Autumn or Winter's days with morning coffee or afternoon tea.

REFERENCE RECIPES

APRICOT SAUCE

INGREDIENTS

3   ROUNDED TABLESPOONS APRICOT JAM
2   LEVEL TABLESPOONS SUGAR
6   TABLESPOONS WHITE WINE

METHOD

Gently heat the jam with the sugar and wine in a small saucepan for about 10 minutes, stirring from time to time to blend thoroughly.

Rub through a sieve to rid the sauce of apricot skin or chunks of peel.

BASIC BREAD RECIPE

INGREDIENTS

1lb   STRONG PLAIN FLOUR
1   TEASPOON SALT
½   TEASPOON SUGAR
½oz   BUTTER OR MARGARINE
½ oz   FRESH YEAST
½   PINT LUKE WARM MILK

METHOD

Into a mixer bowl pour in the milk. Add the sugar and crumble in the fresh yeast. Add the butter or margarine, flour and salt.

Using a dough hook knead all the ingredients together for approximately one minute on a minimum speed.

Increase the speed until a dough is formed, adding a little more flour if the mix is too soft.

Knead for a further 2-3 minutes until the dough is smooth and elastic and leaves the sides of the bowl clean.

Place the dough in a large bowl, cover and leave somewhere warm to double in size – this should take approximately ½ hour.

Return to the mixing bowl and knead again for about 2 minutes.

Place the dough in a greased 1lb. loaf tin, or have fun making different shape loaves, ie cottage loaves or plaits.

Decorate the top by coating with a mixture of egg and milk and sprinkling with poppy, sunflower or sesame seeds.

Leave in a warm place until doubled in size.

HEAT OVEN 220ºC/450ºF/GAS 6

Bake in the oven for approximately 30 minutes.

BRANDY SAUCE
INGREDIENTS

6 floz	MILK
2-3 floz	BRANDY
2	EGG YOLKS
1	LEVEL TEASPOON ARROWROOT OR CORNFLOUR
1	TEASPOON LIGHT BROWN SUGAR

METHOD

Blend the arrowroot or cornflour with a little cold milk.

Heat the remaining milk and when boiling stir it into the blended arrowroot or cornflour.

Return the mixture to the pan and bring back to boiling point.

In a basin mix together the egg yolks, brandy and sugar.

Allow the arrowroot/cornflour sauce to cool a little before whisking into the egg mixture.

Cook (without boiling) whilst whisking until the sauce thickens.

If the mixture appears too thick add a little milk or cream to slacken.

CHOUX ('Shoo') PASTRY
INGREDIENTS

4oz BASIC RECIPE

4oz	PLAIN FLOUR
2oz	BUTTER OR MARGARINE
1	PINT WATER
3	EGGS

METHOD

Place the fat in the water and melt over a gentle heat.
Bring to the boil.

Remove the saucepan from the heat and stir in the flour.

Return to the heat and stir the mixture forms a ball in the middle of the pan.

Allow to cool.

Lightly whisk the eggs and beat thoroughly (adding a little at a time) with a wooden spoon into the cooled mixture.

MAG'S COMMENTS:

**PERFECT RECIPE FOR DORNOCH DREAMS AND OTHER
RECIPES SUCH AS CREAM PUFFS AND ECLAIRS**

FLAKY PASTRY

INGREDIENTS

1lb   PLAIN FLOUR
GOOD PINCH OF SALT
12oz BUTTER OR MARGARINE
      (or equal margarine and lard)
COLD WATER (about ½ pint)
1   TEASPOON LEMON JUICE (optional)

MAG'S TIP:

IF TIME IS LIMITED, KEEP A PACK OF COMMERCIAL FROZEN
FLAKY PASTRY IN THE FREEZER (IT IS A PERFECT STANBY)

METHOD

Mix flour and salt in a bowl.

Divide the fat into four portions.

Rub one portion of fat into the flour.

Add the lemon juice and enough cold water to form an elastic dough, using a knife.

Turn out on to a floured board or work surface and roll out into a rectangle strip. Brush off any surplus flour.

Cover two-thirds of the pastry rectangle with another portion of fat, dotting over the surface in knobs.

Fold the pastry into three by bringing the end without fat to the centre, then folding down the other third.

Press together the pastry edges . Give the pastry half a turn, so that folds are to left and right, and roll out lightly.

Repeat the process twice more to use up the remaining two portions of fat.

Roll out once more and fold up, leaving the pastry in a cold place for an hour before use.

GINGER ICING
INGREDIENTS

4	TABLESPOONS SIFTED ICING SUGAR
1oz	BUTTER
1½	TEASPOONS GROUND GINGER
3	TEASPOONS GOLDEN SYRUP

METHOD

Place all the ingredients in a saucepan over a low heat and stir continuously until blended together and boiling point is reached.

Pour over your chosen cake or biscuits and leave to set.

GLACE` ICING
INGREDIENTS

4oz	SIEVED ICING SUGAR
1	TABLESPOON WARM WATER
FLAVOURING AND COLOURING	

METHOD

Place the icing sugar in a basin.

Add the water.

Stir until smooth.

Add flavour or colouring.

Use at once.

SUGGESTED FLAVOURINGS:

VANILLA ESSENCE
ALMOND ESSENCE
FINELY GRATED ORANGE RIND
and TEASPOON JUICE
FINELY GRATED LEMON RIND
and TEASPOON JUICE

152

HOW TO MAKE THE PERFECT CUP OF TEA

Always use good quality loose leaf or bagged tea.

Always fill the kettle with freshly drawn cold water.

When brewing black and Oolong teas, allow the water to reach boiling point before pouring onto the leaves.

When brewing green tea, boil the water and then allow it to cool slightly before pouring on to the leaves.

Measure the tea carefully into the pot.

Use one tea bag or one rounded teaspoon of loose tea for each cup to be served.

ALLOW THE TEA TO BREW FOR THE CORRECT NUMBER OF MINUTES

Small leafed black tea normally needs 2-3 minutes.

Larger leafed black tea needs 3-5 minutes.

Oolong teas need 5-7 minutes.

Green teas need 1-3 minutes.

It is always advisable where possible, to follow the instructions on packets or test each tea to find the number of minutes that suits.

HOW TO POUR THE TEA

If you are using tea leaves, hold a strainer over the cup to prevent the leaves getting in.

Some people prefer to pour the milk into the cup first, while others prefer after the tea has been poured. The milk should be semi-skimmed, otherwise if the milk is too creamy it spoils the taste of the tea.

HOW TO STEAM A PUDDING

It is simpler to steam puddings in a covered basin but if you wish to try the traditional method, tie the pudding in calico that has been scalded and floured to help seal it, but a characteristic of cloth-boiled puddings is their damp outer crust.

Steaming is most suitable for puddings made with suet pastry, they are lighter and more digestible than when cooked by other methods. This applies to puddings with a suet pastry lining enclosing a filling or to suet mixtures.

Steamed sponge puddings have a more feathery texture than oven baked sponge cakes.

Puddings are covered during steaming to prevent water splashes or steam entering the mixture and making it soggy.

PREPARING THE BASIN

Grease the inside of the basin, using a pastry brush or piece of greaseproof paper.

Place any topping such as jam, sugar, currants, etc at the bottom of the basin.

Fill sponge and suet mixtures to within ½ inch of the top.

Cut out a square of greaseproof paper or aluminium foil for the basin cover and grease one side with a brush.

Place the square greased side down over the top of the basin and make a one inch pleat across the top to allow for expansion of the pudding.

Tie the covering down with fine string wound twice round the basin under the rim, then looped over the top to act as a handle.

JAM SAUCE
INGREDIENTS

3   ROUNDED TABLESPOONS APRICOT JAM – OR JAM OF YOUR CHOICE
2   LEVEL TABLESPOONS SUGAR
6   TABLESPOONS WHITE WINE

METHOD

Gently heat the jam with the sugar and wine in a small saucepan for about 10 minutes, stirring from time to time to blend thoroughly.

Rub through a sieve to rid the sauce of skin or pips.

THE DELICATE FLAVOUR OF FRUIT, CAPTURED IN JAM, COMES
THROUGH THIS SIMPLY MADE SAUCE

SERVE HOT WITH STEAMED SPONGES,
SUET PUDDINGS AND MILK PUDDINGS

LEMON SAUCE

Lemons have always been prized for their health-giving properties, as well as for their flavour and fragrance.

England was slow to appreciate the medicinal value of lemons, but loved their flavour so much that they were used in almost every kind of dish.

The Victorians and Edwardians used them in this sauce, which they served both hot and cold with puddings and plain cake.

Today, it sharpens the flavour of steamed fruit puddings and sponge puddings.

INGREDIENTS

4oz   CASTER SUGAR
1   ROUNDED TABLESPOON CORNFLOUR
¼   TEASPOON SALT
9floz WATER
FINELY GRATED RIND OF 1 LEMON
1oz   BUTTER, CUT INTO SMALL PIECES
3   TABLESPOONS LEMON JUICE

METHOD

Put the sugar, cornflour and salt into a saucepan and stir in the water, a little at a time to make a smooth paste.

Stir in the grated lemon rind and put the pan over a low heat.

Cook gently, stirring continuously until the mixture simmers and thickens.

Continue simmering for about a minute, then remove from the heat.

Beat in the butter pieces one at a time and stir in the lemon juice.

MARMALADE SAUCE
INGREDIENTS

3   ROUNDED TABLESPOONS MARMALADE
2   LEVEL TABLESPOONS SUGAR
6   TABLESPOONS WHITE WINE

SERVE THE SAUCE HOT WITH STEAMED SPONGES, SUET PUDDINGS AND MILK PUDDINGS

METHOD

Gently heat the marmalade with the sugar and wine in a small saucepan for about 10 minutes, stirring from time to time to blend thoroughly.

Rub through a sieve to rid the sauce of any peel.

POACHING FRUIT

Poaching fruit as opposed to stewing, gives a much better result both to eat and to it's appearance, particularly as with a little care it is possible to keep the fruits whole and unbroken.

The syrup is made first and the fruit very gently simmered in it. For a special occasion a little wine, brandy or liqueur can be added.

Soft fruits containing a lot of juice, such as plums, cherries and apricots, require a heavy syrup, but only a little of it.

Hard fruits, such as pears, apples and gooseberries, require a lighter syrup but a greater quantity.

INGREDIENTS
HEAVY SYRUP
4oz SUGAR TO ½ PINT WATER

LIGHT SYRUP
3oz SUGAR TO ½ PINT WATER

If several batches are to be cooked, the syrup may require replenishing. If only a small amount of fruit is poached and too much syrup is left, boil it rapidly with the lid off the pan to reduce a little and to thicken slightly.

METHOD

Place water and sugar in a wide, preferably shallow, pan.

Stir over gentle heat to dissolve sugar and simmer with lid on pan for 2 to 3 minutes.

Wash any fruit to be peeled.

If peeling fruit use a stainless steel knife, peeling the quantity to be poached at one time. Fruit which discolours easily – pears, apples etc keep a better colour if a teaspoon of lemon juice is added to the syrup.

Place the prepared fruit into the syrup in one layer and simmer very gently with lid on pan until tender. Time will vary according to the ripeness of the fruit.

Lift the fruit carefully into a serving bowl and repeat the process until the required quantity of fruit is cooked.

Add the odd teaspoon of wine, brandy or liqueur to the syrup and pour over the fruit.

Serve when cold.

SHORT PASTRY
INGREDIENTS

1lb	SELF RAISING FLOUR
1	TEASPOON SALT
4oz	LARD
4oz	MARGARINE
	COLD WATER (for mixing)
2oz	CASTER SUGAR
	(optional for sweet pastry)

Mag's comments:
If available, I like to use
'golden jewel flour'.
White Flora can be used instead of
lard and butter instead of margarine
if you wish. Being a person of the 'modern world'
I confess to nearly always making my pastry
in the food processor.

METHOD

Mix the flour and salt in a basin.

Rub in the lard and margarine.

Using a knife to cut and stir, mix with cold water to form a stiff paste.

Turn the pastry on to a floured board or worktop to roll out.

Plain short pastry can be used for making flan cases, but if a sweet filling is required, add sugar to the pastry.

BAKE 'BLIND'
Line flan ring or dish with rolled out pastry.

Place a circle of bakewell paper over the pastry, then a layer of rice or ceramic beans (store in a jar for future use).

If the case is for immediate use, with a hot filling, bake for 15 minutes. Remove rice or beans, and paper. Fill and return to the oven.

When making a case for a cold filling, or to store for future use, bake for 20 minutes. Remove the beans and flan ring, then return to the oven for a further 5 minutes until crisp and firm.

SUET CRUST PASTRY

Suet crust pastry is a traditional British pastry used in the making of steamed and boiled pudding, roly-poly puddings and dumplings. The fillings or toppings can be sweet or savoury.

INGREDIENTS

8oz	SELF RAISING FLOUR
4oz	SHREDDED/CHOPPED SUET OR VEGETARIAN ALTERNATIVE
	PINCH OF SALT
	COLD WATER

METHOD

Sieve the flour and salt into a large bowl.

Add the suet and mix lightly.

Mix with sufficient water to make a soft, but firm, dough.

Turn out on to a lightly floured work surface.

Knead gently until smooth.

USE FOR SWEET OR SAVOURY, STEAMED OR BAKED DISHES

SWEET YEAST DOUGH

INGREDIENTS

1oz   FRESH YEAST
5floz WARM WATER (1 part boiling to 2 parts cold)
1lb   PLAIN FLOUR
½   TEASPOON SALT
2oz   CASTER SUGAR
4oz   MARGARINE
2   EGGS

METHOD

Cream the yeast with a little warm water.

Mix flour, salt and sugar in a bowl.

Rub in the margarine.

Add the yeast liquid and beaten eggs to the flour and knead well.

Leave to rise in a warm place for 45-60 minutes.

Turn the dough on to a floured surface and knead again lightly.

Shape and bake as required.

USE THIS RECIPE TO MAKE DEVONSHIRE SPLITS,
CHELSEA BUNS, DOUGHNUTS, HOT CROSS BUNS
AND FRUIT TEA LOAVES